NEW LIBERTARIAN MANIFESTO

The accumulated works of
Samuel Edward Konkin III
are available at
kopubco.com

NEW LIBERTARIAN MANIFESTO

by

Samuel Edward Konkin III

Fourth (25th Anniversary) Edition, August 2006

ISBN 10 0-9777649-2-3
ISBN 13 978-0-9777649-2-1

Published by arrangement with the author.

KoPubCo
publishing division of The Triplanetary Corporation
5942 Edinger Ave., Ste. 113-164
Huntington Beach, California 92649
www.kopubco.com

KOPUBCO and the KoPubCo and Triplanetary colophons are trademarks of the Triplanetary Corporation.

Printed by Lightning Source, Inc.

First edition published by Anarchosamisdat Press, Los Angeles, 1980

Second edition published by KoPubCo, Los Angeles, 1983

Third (Memorial) Edition published by Foundation for Social Justice, March 28, 2004

Cover designed by Black Dawn Graphics

Dedication

To Chris R. Tame
who told me
*"Don't get it right,
get it written!"*

Acknowledgments
above all to
Ludwig Von Mises,
Murray N. Rothbard,
Robert LeFevre,
and *their* sources.

Samuel Edward Konkin III
July 8, 1947—February 23, 2004

CRITIQUES OF *NEW LIBERTARIAN MANIFESTO*

NEW LIBERTARIAN MANIFESTO

PREFACE TO THE FIRST EDITION

The basic form of New Libertarianism arose during my struggle with the Libertarian Party during its formation in 1973, and Counter-Economics was first put forward to the public at the Free Enterprise Forum in Los Angeles in February 1974. New Libertarianism has been propagated within and without the libertarian movement and its journals, most notably *New Libertarian* magazine, since then.

More important, the activism prescribed herein (especially CounterEconomics) has been practiced by the author and his closest allies since 1976. Several "anarchovillages" of New Libertarians have formed and reformed.

Just once, wouldn't you like to read a manifesto that's been practiced before it's preached? I wanted to.

And I did it.

—Samuel Edward Konkin III
October 1980

PREFACE TO THE SECOND EDITION

An agorist publication ought to be judged most severely in the free marketplace. Sure enough, the first edition of *New Libertarian Manifesto* has been sold out and a second edition, taken up by a fresh entrepreneur looking for profit with his ideology, is with you, the reader. The market's judgment, to my pleasant surprise, is that *NLM* is the most successful of my many publications.

In the realm of ideas, two years is a fairly short time. Nevertheless, attacks on *NLM* have begun in Left-Centre Libertarian publications and one such student network newsletter berated errant chapters for switching allegiance to "that flake, Konkin" only last month. Essays and articles on Counter-Economics and agorism appear in more and more non-Left (or non-agorist—yet) libertarian publications.

A truly encouraging sign is the emergence of many Counter-Economic entrepreneurs in the Southern California area (and a few scattered around North America and even Europe) who embrace and distribute *NLM*. An agorist "industrial park" has been condensing quietly in Orange County between these two editions.

This gratification is not idly enjoyed. It has inspired the author to continue the dialogue in two issues of a theoretical journal based on *NLM*, the writing of *Counter-Economics* (see footnote 26), and the planning of a theoretical magnum opus, as *Das Capital* was to the *Communist Manifesto*, undoubtedly to be titled *Agorism*.

As for continuing to practice what I preach and expanding on the practice, I may add to the end of the First Preface...

And I'm still doing it.

—Samuel Edward Konkin III
February, 1983

PREFACE TO THE FOURTH EDITION

Samuel Edward Konkin III had suggested that—instead of updating the Manifesto with new notes—we simply publish it as is, as an historical piece of living theory that continues to grow to this day. The only changes have been the correction of some persistent typos and minor changes for the sake of clarity made by the editor. Mr. Konkin joined the great anarchist hoard in the sky on February 23, 2004, after a too-short lifetime of theoretical and practical experiments, traveling the world to bring the concept of agorism and New Libertarianism to eager listeners.

Twenty-five years after its publication, the Manifesto is still a brisk seller. This on-demand edition—available worldwide—should continue the trend.

With the collapse of collectivism sweeping the world—a collapse brought about by the economic and moral consequences of such systems—Mr. Konkin's analyses are all the more impressive for their accuracy. If anything, *New Libertarian Manifesto* is more current now than ever. Statism choked and died in the USSR. The UN as proto-World State is collapsing into toothless, impotent irrelevance. Will inhabitants of the world continue the trend, or do we need the frontier of Space to achieve the next evolutionary step in human action?

The Movement of the Libertarian Left can be contacted at agorism.info and all back issues of *New Libertarian* publications are available from KoPubCo at kopubco.com.

—**Victor Koman**
Publisher
March, 2006

I. STATISM: OUR CONDITION

We are coerced by our fellow human beings. Since they have the ability to choose to do otherwise, our condition need not be this. Coercion is immoral, inefficient, and unnecessary for human life and fulfillment. Those who wish to be supine as their neighbors prey on them are free so to choose; this manifesto is for those who choose otherwise: to fight back.

To combat coercion, one must understand it. More important, one must understand what one is fighting *for* as much as what one is fighting *against*. Blind reaction goes in all directions negative to the source of oppression and disperses opportunity; pursuit of a common goal focuses the opponents and allows formation of coherent strategy and tactics.

Diffuse coercion is optimally handled by local, immediate self-defense. Though the market may develop larger-scale businesses for protection and restoration, random threats of violence can only be dealt with on the spot *ad hoc.*[1]

Organized coercion requires organized opposition. (An excellent case has been made many times by many thinkers that such organization should remain skeletal at best, fleshing out only for actual confrontation, in order to prevent perversion of the defenders into an

---

[1]I am indebted to Robert LeFevre for this insight, though we draw differing conclusions.

agency of aggression.) Institutional coercion, developed over the millennia with roots of mysticism and delusion planted deep in the victims' thinking, requires a grand strategy and a cataclysmic point of historical singularity: Revolution.

Such an institution of coercion—centralizing immorality, directing theft and murder, and coordinating oppression on a scale inconceivable by random criminality—exists. It is the Mob of mobs, Gang of gangs, Conspiracy of conspiracies. It has murdered more people in a few recent years than all the deaths in history before that time; it has stolen in a few recent years more than all the wealth produced in history to that time; it has deluded—for its survival—more minds in a few recent years than all the irrationality in history to that time; Our Enemy, The State.[2]

In the 20th Century alone, war has murdered more than all previous deaths; taxes and inflation have stolen more than all wealth previously produced; and the political lies, propaganda, and above all, "Education," have twisted more minds than all the superstition prior: yet through all the deliberate confusion and obfuscation, the thread of reason has developed fibers of resistance to be woven into the rope of execution for the State: Libertarianism.

Where the State divides and conquers its opposition, Libertarianism unites and liberates. Where the State beclouds, Libertarianism clarifies; where the State conceals, Lib-

---

[2]Thank you, Albert J. Nock, for that phrase.

ertarianism uncovers; where the State pardons, Libertarianism accuses.

Libertarianism elaborates an entire philosophy from one simple premise: initiatory violence or its threat (coercion) is wrong (immoral, evil, bad, supremely impractical, etc.) and is forbidden; nothing else is.[3]

Libertarianism, as developed to this point, discovered the problem and defined the solution: the State *vs.* the Market. The Market is the sum of all *voluntary* human action.[4] If one acts non-coercively, one is part of the Market. Thus did Economics become part of Libertarianism.

Libertarianism investigated the nature of man to explain his rights deriving from non-coercion. It immediately followed that man (woman, child, Martian, etc.) had an absolute right to this life and other property—and no right to the life or property of others. Thus did Objective philosophy become part of Libertarianism.

Libertarianism asked why society was not libertarian now and found the State, its ruling class, its camouflage, and the heroic historians striving to reveal the truth. Thus did Revisionist History become part of Libertarianism.

Psychology, especially as developed by Thomas Szasz as counter-psychology, was embraced by libertarians seeking to free them-

---

[3]Modern Libertarianism is best explained by Murray Rothbard in *For A New Liberty*, which, regardless how recent the edition, is always a year or more out of date. Recommending even the best writing on libertarianism is like recommending one song to explain music in all its forms.

[4]Thank you, Ludwig Von Mises.

selves from both State restraint and self-imprisonment. Seeking an art form to express the horror potential of the State and extrapolate the many possibilities of liberty, Libertarianism found Science Fiction already in the field.

From the political, economic, philosophical, psychological, historical, and artistic realms the partisans of liberty saw a whole, integrating their resistance with others elsewhere, and they came together as their consciousness became aware. Thus did Libertarians become a Movement.

The Libertarian Movement looked around and saw the challenge: everywhere, Our Enemy, The State; from the ocean's depth past arid desert outposts to the distant lunar surface; in every land, people, tribe, and nation—and in the individual mind.

Some sought immediate alliance with other opponents of the power elite to overthrow the State's present rulers.[5] Some sought immediate confrontation with the State's agents.[6] Some pursued collaboration with those in power who offered less oppression in exchange for votes.[7] And some dug in for long-term enlightenment of the populace to build and develop the Movement.[8] Everywhere, a Libertar-

---

[5] Radical Libertarian Alliance, 1968-71

[6] Radical Libertarian Action Movement, 1968-72, later revived briefly as a proto-MLL.

[7] Citizens for a Restructured Republic, 1972, made up of RLA members disillusioned with revolution.

[8] Society for Individual Liberty, 1969-89 (Now merged with Libertarian International to the International Society for Individual Liberty). Also Rampart College (now defunct) and the Foundation for Economic Education and Free Enterprise Institute, all of whom were around before the libertarian population explosion of 1969.

ian Alliance of activists sprang up.[9]

The State's Higher Circles were not about to yield their plunder and restore property to their victims at the first sign of opposition. The first counterattack came from anti-principles already planted by the corrupt Intellectual Caste: Defeatism, Retreatism, Minarchism, Collaborationism, Gradualism, Monocentrism, and Reformism—including accepting State office to "improve" Statism! All of these anti-principles (deviations, heresies, self-destructive contradictory tenets, etc.) will be dealt with later. Worst of all is Partyarchy, the anti-concept of pursuing libertarian ends through statist means, especially political parties.

A "Libertarian" Party was the second counterattack of the State unleashed on the fledgling Libertarians, first as a ludicrous oxymoron,[10] then as an invading army.[11]

---

[9] Most important, the California Libertarian Alliance, 1969-73. The name is still kept alive for sponsorship of conferences, and is also used in the United Kingdom.

[10] The first "Libertarian" Party was set up by Gabriel Aguilar and Ed Butler in California in 1970 as a hollow shell to gain media access. (Aguilar, a Galambosian, was staunchly anti-political.) Even Nolan's "L"P was mocked and scorned by such as Murray Rothbard in the first year of its existence.

[11] The "Libertarian" Party that eventually organized nationally and ran John Hospers and Toni Nathan for President and Vice-President in 1972 was first organized by David and Susan Nolan in December 1971 in Colorado. Dave Nolan was a Massachusetts YAFer who had broken with YAF back in 1967 and missed the 1969 climax at St. Louis. He remained conservative and minarchist right up to this first edition.

Although the Nolans were rather innocent, and other early organization and candidates often so, the debate

The third counterattack was an attempt by one of the ten richest capitalists in the United States to buy the major Libertarian institutions—not just the Party—and run the movement as other plutocrats run all other political parties in capitalist states.[12]

The degree of success those statist counterattacks had in corrupting libertarianism led to a splintering of the Movement's "Left" and

---

on "the Party Question" began immediately. *New Libertarian Notes* attacked the "L"P concept in Spring 1972 and ran a debate between Nolan and Konkin just before the election (*NLN 15*).

By the 1980 presidential campaign, the Nolans had broken with the "L"P leadership of Ed Crane and his candidate Ed Clark, who ran a high-powered, high-financed, traditional vote-chasing and platform-trimming campaign.

[12] Charles G. Koch—Wichita oil billionaire—through his relatives, foundations, institutes, and centers, had set up, bought up, or "bought out" the following from 1976-79: Murray Rothbard and his *Libertarian Forum*; *Libertarian Review* (from Robert Kephart), edited by Roy A. Childs; Students for a Libertarian Society (SLS), run by Milton Mueller; Center for Libertarian Studies (Rothbard-leaning) and Joe Peden; *Inquiry*, edited by Williamson Evers; Cato Institute; and various Koch Funds, Foundations, and Institutes. Named the "Kochtopus" in *New Libertarian 1* (February 1978), it was first attacked in print by Edith Efron in the conservative-libertarian publication *Reason*, along with allegations of an "anarchist" conspiracy. The Movement of the Libertarian Left cut away Efron's anti-anarchist ravings and rushed to support her on her key revelation of the growth of *monocentrism* in the Movement.

In 1979, the Kochtopus took control of the National Libertarian party at the Los Angeles convention. David Koch, Charles' brother, openly bought the VP nomination for $500,000.

the despairing paralyzation of others. As disillusionment grew within "Libertarianism," the disillusioned sought answers to this new problem: the State *within* as well as the State without. How do we avoid being used by the State and its power elite? That is, they asked, how can we avoid deviations from the path of liberty when we *know* there are more than one? The market has many paths to production and consumption of a product and none are perfectly predictable. So even if one tells us how to get from here (statism) to there (liberty), how do we know *that* is the best way?

Already some are dredging up the old strategies of movements long dead, movements with other goals. New paths are indeed being offered—back to the State.[13]

Betrayal, inadvertent or planned, continues. It need not.

While no one can predict the sequence of steps that will unerringly achieve a free society for free-willed individuals, one can eliminate in one slash all those that will *not* advance Liberty, and applying the principles of

---

[13] Murray Rothbard broke with the Kochtopus soon after the '79 LP Convention and most of his close allies were purged, such as Williamson Evers of *Inquiry*. CLS was cut off from Koch funding. The *Libertarian Forum* began attacking Koch. Rothbard and young Justin Raimondo set up a new "radical" caucus of the LP (the first one, 1972-74, was run by progenitors of NLA as a recruiting tactic and as a way to destroy the Party from within).

Although Rothbard was moved to ask "Is Sam Konkin Right?" in his July 1980 speech to an RC dinner in Orange County, the RC strategy is to reform the LP using New Left and neo-Marxist tactics.

the Market unwaveringly map out a terrain to travel. There is no One Way, one straight line graph to Liberty, to be sure. But there is a family of graphs, a Space filled with lines, that will take the libertarian to his goal of the free society, and that Space can be described.

Once the goal is fixed and the paths discovered, only the Action of the individual to go from here to there remains. Above all, this manifesto calls for that Action.[14]

---

[14] I hope subsequent editions may omit this note, but in the present historical context it is vital to point out that Libertarianism is *not* specifically for the most "advanced" or enlightened elements of North America, perhaps typified by the young, white, highly read computer consultant, equally feminist mate (and 0.5 children). Only the freest market can raise the "Second" and "Third World" from grinding poverty and self-destructive superstition. Compulsory attempts critically to raise production standards and associated cultural understanding have caused backlash and regression: e.g. Iran and Afghanistan. Mostly, the State has engaged in deliberate repression of self-improvement.

Quasi-free markets, such as the freeports of Hong Kong, Singapore, and (earlier) Shanghai, attracted floods of upwardly mobile, highly motivated entrepreneurs. The incredibly well-developed black market of Burma already runs the entire economy and needs only a libertarian awareness to oust Ne Win and the Army, accelerating trade and annihilating poverty overnight.

Similar observations are possible about developed black markets and tolerated semi-free markets in the "Second World" of Soviet occupation, such as Armenia, Georgia, and the Russian counter-economy (*nalevo*)

Note to Second Edition: The above note is still, sadly enough, needed.

Note to Third Edition: With the collapse of Communism, maybe the need is declining, but the note's still here!

II. Agorism: Our Goal

The basic principle that leads a libertarian from statism to a free society is the same that the founders of libertarianism used to discover the theory itself. That principle is *consistency*. Thus, consistent application of the theory of libertarianism to every action the individual libertarian takes creates the libertarian society.

Many thinkers have expressed the need for consistency between means and ends and not all were libertarians. Ironically, many statists have claimed *inconsistency* between laudable ends and contemptible means; yet when their true ends of greater power and oppression were understood, their means are found to be quite consistent. It is part of the statist mystique to confuse the necessity of ends-means consistency; it is thus the most crucial activity of the libertarian theorist to expose inconsistencies. Many theorists have done so admirably; but few have attempted and most failed to describe the consistent means and ends combination of libertarianism.[15]

---

[15] To cite the most spectacular so far:

- Murray Rothbard will use any past political strategy to further libertarianism, falling back on ever more radical ones when the previous ones fail.
- Robert LeFevre advocates a purity of thought and deed in each individual that this author and many others find inspiring. But he holds back from describing a

Whether or not this manifesto is itself correct can be determined by the same principle. If consistency fails, then all within is meaningless; in fact, language is then gibberish and existence a fraud. This cannot be overemphasized. Should an inconsistency be discovered in these pages, then *the consistent reformulation is New Libertarianism*, not what has been found in error. New Libertarianism (*agorism*) *cannot* be discredited without Liberty or Real-

---

complete strategy resulting from these personal tactics, partially due to a fear of being charged with *prescribing* as well as *describing*. This author has no such fear. LeFevre's pacifism also dilutes the attraction of his libertarian tactics, probably far more than deserved.

• Andrew J. Galambos advocates a fairly counter-economic position (see the next chapter) but positively drives away recruits by his anti-movement stance and his "secret society" organizational tactic. His "primary property" deviationism, like LeFevre's pacifism, probably also detracts from the rest of his theory more than is warranted.

• Harry Browne's *How I Found Freedom in an Unfree World* is an immensely popular guide to personal liberation. Having been influenced by Rothbard, LeFevre, and Galambos, Browne fairly correctly—if superficially—maps out valid tactics for the individual to survive and prosper in a statist society. He offers no overall strategy, and his techniques would break down in an advanced counter-economic system as it nears the free society.

• A deviation with no particular spokesperson but associated largely with the *Libertarian Connection* is the idea of achieving freedom by outflanking the State with technology. This seems to have plausible validity in the recent case of the U.S. State deciding not to regulate the explosive-growth information industry. But it fails to take into account the ingenuity of those who will keep statism around as long as people demand it.

•

ity (or both) being discredited, only an incorrect formulation.

Let us begin by sighting our goal. What does a free society look like, or at least a society as free as we can hope to achieve with our present understanding?[16]

Undoubtedly the freest society yet envisioned is that of Robert LeFevre. All relations between people are voluntary exchanges—a free market. No one will injure another or trespass in any way.

Of course, a lot more than statism would have to be eliminated from individual consciousness for his society to exist. Most damaging of all to this perfectly free society is its lack of a mechanism of correction.[17] All it takes is a handful of practitioners of coercion to enjoy their ill-gotten plunder in enough company to sustain them—and freedom is dead. Even if all are living free, one "bite of the apple," one throwback, reading old history or rediscovering evil on his own, will "unfree" the perfect society.

The next-best-thing to a free society is the Libertarian society. Eternal vigilance is the price of Liberty (Thomas Jefferson) and it may be possible to have a small number of individuals in

---

[16] When our understanding increases, one assumes we can achieve a freer society.

[17] In *The Great Explosion*, SF writer Eric Frank Russell posits a society close to that envisioned by LeFevre. The pacifist Gands did have a correction mechanism for occasionally aberrant individuals—the "Idle Jack" cases. Unfortunately, shunning would fail the moment the coercers reached a "critical number" to form a supportive, self-sustaining sub-society. That they could is obvious—they have!

the marketplace ready to defend against sporadic aggression. Or large numbers may retain sufficient knowledge and ability to use that knowledge of basic self-defense to deter random attacks (the coercer never knowing who might be well-versed in defense) and eliminate the profitability of systematic violence initiation.

Even so, there remain two problems inordinately difficult for this system of "Anarchy with spontaneous defense." First is the problem of defending those who are noticeably defenseless. This can be reduced by advanced technology to people who are quadriplegic morons (assuming *that* won't be solved by sufficient technology) and very young children who require constant attention anyway. Then there are those who for a brief time go defenseless and the even rarer cases of those who are overwhelmed by violence initiators wishing to test their skills against a probably weaker foe. (The last is most rare simply because of the high risk and low material return on investment.)

Those who need not—and should not—be defended are those who consciously choose not to be: pacifists. LeFevre and his disciples need never fear some Libertarian will use methods they find repugnant to defend them. (Perhaps they can wear a "dove" button for quick recognition?)

Far more important is what to do with the violence initiator after defence. The case in which one's property is violated successfully and one is not there to protect it comes readily to mind. And finally, though actually a special case of the above, is the possibility of fraud and other forms of contract violation.[18]

These cases may be settled by the primitive "shoot-out" or socially—that is, through the intervention of a third party who has no vested interest in either of the two parties to the dispute. This case is the fundamental problem of society.[19]

Any attempts to force a solution against the wishes of both parties violates Libertarian principle. So a "shoot-out" involving no risk to third parties is acceptable—but hardly profitable or efficient or even civilized (aesthetically pleasing) save to a few cultists.

The solution, then, requires a judge, "Fair Witness," or arbitrator. Once an arbitrator to a dispute or judge of an aggression has performed judgment and communicated the decision, enforcement may be required. (Pacifists may choose arbitration without enforcement, by the way.)

The following market system has been proposed by Rothbard, Linda and Morris Tannehill, and others; it need not be defini-

---

[18] The Mises-Rothbard position that fraud and failure to fulfill contract (the latter may be taken care of by clauses in the contract, of course) is itself theft: of *future* goods. The basis of contract is the transfer of present goods (consideration here and now) for future goods (consideration there and then).

All theft is violence initiation; force is used to take property away involuntarily or to prevent receipt of goods or payment for goods freely transferred by agreement.

[19] Society, as Mises points out, exists because of the advantages of division of labor. By specializing in different steps of production, individuals find total wealth produced greater than by their individual efforts.

tive and may be improved by advances in theory and technology (as this author has already done). At this stage of history, it seems optimal and is presented here as the beginning working model.

First, always leaving out those who choose not to participate, one insures oneself against aggression or theft. One can even assign a value to one's life in case of murder (or inadvertent manslaughter) which may range from the taking of the violence-initiator's life, taking replaceable organs (technology willing) to restore the victim's life, to paying a foundation to continue one's life's work. What is crucial here is that the victim assigns the value to his life, body, and property *before* the mishap. (Exchangeable goods may simply be replaced at market rate. See below.)

A finds property missing and reports it to insurance company IA. IA investigates (either through another division or through a separate detective agency D). IA promptly replaces the object to A so that loss of use of the good is minimized.[20] D now may fail to discover the missing property. In that case, the loss to IA is covered by the premiums paid for the insur-

---

[20] At this point we must introduce Mises' concept of *time-preference.* Future goods are always discounted relative to present goods because of the *use-time* foregone. While individual valuations of time-preference vary, those with high time-preference can borrow from those with lower time-preference since the high-preferrers will pay more to the low-preferrers than the value they have foregone. The point where all these transactions of time-preference clear on the free market defines the basic or *originary rate of interest* for all loans and capital investment.

ance. Note well that in order to keep premiums low and competitive, IA has a strong incentive to maximize retrieval of stolen or lost goods. (One could wax eloquent for volumes on the lack of such incentive for monopoly detective systems such as State police forces, and their horrendous social cost.)

If D does discover the goods, say in B's possession, and B freely returns them (perhaps induced by reward), the case is closed. Only if B claims property right in the object also claimed by A does conflict arise.

B retains insurance company IB, which may perform its own independent investigation and convince IA that D erred. Failing that, IA and IB are now in conflict. At this point, the standard objections to market anarchy have been brought up that the "war" between A and B has been enlarged to include large insurance companies which may have sizeable protection divisions or contracts with protection companies (PA and PB). But wherein lies the incentive for IA and IB to use violence and destroy not only its competitor's assets but surely at least some of its own? They have even less incentive in a market society long established; the companies have specialists and capital tied up in defense. Any company investing in *offense* would become highly suspect and surely lose customers in a predominantly Libertarian society (which is what is under discussion).

Very cheaply and profitably, IA and IB can simply pay an arbitration company to settle the dispute, presenting their respective claims and evidence. If B has rightful claim, IA drops the case, taking its small loss (compared to war!) and has excellent incentive to improve its investigation. If A has rightful claim, the reverse is now true for IB.

Only at this point, when the matter has been fully contested, investigated, and judged, and *still* B refuses to relinquish the stolen property, would violence occur. (B may have only been bothered so far as being notified of IB's defense on B's behalf, and B may have chosen to ignore it; no subpœnæ could be issued until *after* conviction.) But PB and IB step aside and B must now face a competent, efficient team of specialists in recovery of stolen property. Even if B is near-mad in his resistance at this point, he would probably be neutralized with minimum fuss by a market agency eager for a good public image and more customers—including B himself some day. Above all, PA must act so as not to invade anyone else or harm the property of *others*.

B or IB is now liable for *restoration*. This can be divided into three parts: restitution, time preference, and apprehension.

Restitution is the return of the original good or its market equivalent. This could be applied even to parts of the human body or the value set on one's life.

Time-preference is the restitution for the time-use lost and is easily determined by the market rate of interest which IA had to pay immediately to restore A's property.

Apprehension is the sum of the cost of investigation, detection, arbitration, and enforcement. Note well how the market works to give B a high incentive to restore the loot quickly to minimize apprehension cost (exactly the opposite to most statist systems) and to minimize interest accrued.

Finally, note all the built-in incentives for swift, efficient justice and restoration with a minimum of fuss and violence. Contrast this with all other systems *in operation*; note as well that *in parts* all this system has been tried successfully throughout history. Only the whole is new and exclusive to Libertarian theory.

This model of restoration has been spelled out so specifically, even though it may be improved and developed, because it solves the only social problem involving any violence whatsoever. The rest of this Libertarian society can be best pictured by imaginative science-fiction authors with a good grounding in praxeology (Mises' term for the study of human action, especially, but not only, economics).

Some hallmarks of this society—libertarian in theory and free-market in practice, called *agorist*, from the Greek *agora*, meaning "open marketplace"—are rapid innovation in science, technology, communication, transportation, production, and distribution. A complementary case can be made for rapid innovation and development in the arts and humanities to keep up with the more material progress; also, such non-material progress would be likely because of total liberty in all forms of nonviolent artistic expression and ever more rapid and complete communication of it to willing recipients. The libertarian literature extolling these benefits of freedom is already a large body and growing rapidly.

One must conclude this description of restoration theory by dealing with some of the arcane objections to it. Most of these reduce to challenges to ascribe value to violated goods or persons. Letting the impersonal market *and the victim* decide seems most fair to both victim *and aggressor*.

The latter point offends some who feel *punishment* is required for evil in thought; reversibility of deed is not enough for them.[21]

Though none of them has come up with a moral basis for punishment, Rothbard and

---

[21] Murray Rothbard takes the most moderate position here: he advocates double restoration; that is, not only must the aggressor restore the victim to prior unharmed condition (as much as possible), but must become himself a victim for an equivalent amount! Not only does this doubling seem arbitrary, nowhere does Rothbard provide a moral basis for punishment, let alone a "moral calculus" (*a la* Bentham).

Others are far worse in demanding ever-greater plunder of the apprehended aggressor, making it probable that only the grossest fool who happened to err momentarily would ever turn himself in, and would, rather, attempt to cost his pursuers dearly. Many neo-Randists would shoot a child for purloining a candy (Gary Greenberg, for instance); others have chained teenagers to their beds to work off trivial trespasses.

This is yet brushing the tip of horror. Far greater a travesty of justice is proposed by those who do not wish to restitute or even mildly punish but to *rehabilitate* the violence-initiator. While some of the more enlightened among the rehabilitators would accept concurrent working off of restitution debt, they would seize upon the victim's delegation of right of self-defense (the basis of all legal action) to incarcerate and brainwash the now-helpless apprehended aggressor.

Not content with punishing the person, scourging the body, and perhaps even inflicting the relative mercy of cruel physical torture, rehabilitators seek the destruction of values and motivation; that is, the annihilation of the Ego. In more florid but well-deserved language, they wish to *devour the soul* of the apprehended aggressor!

David Friedman in particular argue for the economic necessity of deterrence. They argue that *any* percentage of apprehension less than 100% allows a small probability of success; hence, a "rational criminal" may choose to take the risk for his gain. Thus, additional deterrence must be added in the form of punishment. That this also will decrease the incentive for the aggressor to turn himself in and thus lower further the rate of apprehension is not considered, or perhaps the punishment is to be escalated at ever-faster rates to beat the accelerating rate of evasion. As this is written, the *lowest* rate of evasion from state-defined crimes is 80%; most criminals have better than 90% chance of not being caught. This is within a punishment-rehabilitation system wherein no restoration occurs (the victim being further plundered by taxation to support the penal system) and the market is banished. Small wonder there is a thriving "red market" in non-State violence initiation!

Even so, this criticism of agorist restoration fails to note that there is an "entropy" factor. The potential aggressor must put the gain of the object of theft against the loss of the object *plus* interest *plus* apprehension cost. It is true that if he turns himself in immediately, the latter two are minimal—but so are the costs to the victim and insurer.

Not only is agorist restoration happily deterrent in a reciprocal relation with compliance, but the market cost of the apprehension factor allows a precise quantifiable measurement of the social cost of coercion in society. No other proposed system known to this time does that. As most libertarians have been saying, freedom works.

Nowhere in agorist restoration theory do the thoughts of the aggressor enter into the picture. The aggressor is assumed only to be a human actor and responsible for his actions. Furthermore, what business is it of anyone else what anyone thinks? What is relevant is what the aggressor does. Thought is not action; in thought, at least, anarchy remains absolute.[22]

If you sit up in shock to find that I have crashed through your picture window, you don't particularly care if I tripped and fell through while walking by or if I engaged in some act of irrational anger jumping through or even whether it was a premeditated plan to distract protectors across the street from a noticing a bank heist. What you want is your window back *pronto* (and the mess cleared). *What I think is irrelevant to your restoration.* In fact, it can be easily demonstrated that even the smallest expenditure of energy on this subject is pure waste. Motivation—or *suspected* motivation, which is all we can know[22]—may be relevant to detection and even to prove plausibility of the aggressor's action to an arbitrator if there may be two equally probable suspects, but all that matters for justice—as a libertarian sees it—is that the victim has been restored to a condition as identical as

---

[22] Should telepathy be discovered and practically achievable, it may at least then be *possible* to investigate motive and intent; still, the only use in an agorist system would be for mercy pleas—mercy at the further expense of the victim. This footnote is also relevant to the following paragraph which is why it is twice denoted.

possible to pre-harm. Let God or conscience punish "guilty thoughts."[23]

Another objection raised concerns what will be done about violence initiators who have paid their debt (to the individual, *not* "society"), and are "free" to try again—with greater experience. What about recidivism, so prevalent in statist society?

Of course, once one is marked as an aggressor, one will probably be watched more closely and thought of first when a similar crime is committed. And while work camps may be used to repay restitution in a few extreme cases, most aggressors will be allowed to work in relative freedom on bond. Thus no "institutions of criminal higher learning" such as prisons will be around to educate and encourage aggression.

The distinguishing characteristic of a highly efficient and accurate system of judgment and protection will be that it will occupy a negligible fraction of an individual's time, thought, or money. One can then argue that we have not portrayed 99% of the agorist society at all.

---

[23] A good question is: where did "punishment" ever get started? The concept is applicable only to slaves who have nothing else to lose but the lack of pain; to the utterly worthless if any exist; and to very young children who are incapable of paying for restoration and are considered inadequately responsible to incur debt. Of course, a primitive economy generally had far too many problems with rationality and technology to provide much trustworthy detection and measurement of value.

Still, some primitive societies such as the Irish, Icelandic, and Ibo introduced systems of repayment to meliorate vengeance—and promptly evolved into quasi-anarchies.

What about elimination of self-destruction (which Libertarianism does not deal with), space exploration and colonization, life extension, intelligence increase, interpersonal relations, and aesthetic variations? All that really can and *need be* said is that where present man must spend half or more of his time and energy serving or resisting the State, that time-energy (physicist definition of action) will be usable for all other aspects of self-improvement and harnessing of nature. It takes a cynical view of humanity indeed to imagine anything but a richer, happier society.

This then is a sketch of our goal and a detailed picture or enlarged focus on the aspect of justice and protection. We have the "here" and the "there." Now for the path—Counter-Economics.

III. Counter-Economics: Our Means

Having detailed our past and statist present and glimpsed a credible view of a far better society achievable with present understanding and technology—no change in human nature needed—we come to the critical part of the manifesto: how do we get from here to there? The answer breaks naturally—or maybe unnaturally—into two parts. Without a State, a differentiation into *micro* (manipulation of an individual by himself and his environment—including the market) and the *macro* (manipulation of collectives) would be at best an interesting statistical exercise with some small reference to marketing agencies. Even so, a person with a highly sophisticated decency may wish to understand the *social* consequences of his or her acts even if they harm no other.

With a State tainting every act and befouling our minds with unearned guilt, it becomes extremely important to understand the social consequences of our acts. For example, if we fail to pay a tax and get away with it, who is hurt? Us? The State? Innocents? Libertarian analysis shows us that the *State* is responsible for any damage to innocents it alleges that the "selfish tax-evader" has incurred; and the "services" the State "provides" us are illusory. But even so, must there not be more than lonely resistance cleverly concealed or "dropping out"? If a political party or revolutionary army is inappropriate and self-defeating for libertarian goals, what sort of collective action works?

The answer is *agorism*.

It is possible, practical, and even profitable to entrepreneur large collections of humanity away from statist society to the agora. This is, in the deepest sense, true revolutionary activity and will be covered in the next chapter. To understand this *macro* answer, however, we must first outline the *micro* answer.[24]

The function of the pseudo-science of Establishment economics, even more than making predictions for the ruling class (as did the Imperial Roman augurs), is to mystify and confuse the ruled class as to where their wealth is going and how it is taken. An explanation of how people can keep their wealth and property safe from the State, then, is Counter-Establishment economics, or Counter-Economics[25] for short. The actual practice of human actions that evade, avoid, and

---

[24] *Micro* and *macro* are terms from present Establishment economics. While Counter-Economics is part of *agorism* (until the State is gone), agorism includes both Counter-Economics in practice and libertarianism in theory. Since that theory includes an awareness of the consequences of large-scale Counter-Economic practice, I will use *agorist* in this macro sense and *counter-economic* in the micro sense. Since the division is inherently ambiguous, some overlap and interchangeability will occur.

[25] The term "Counter-Economics" was formed the same way as the term "counter-culture;" it does not mean anti-economic science any more than counter-culture meant anti-culture.

defy the State is counter-economic activity, but—in the same sloppy way that "economics" refers both to the science and what it studies—"counter-economics" will undoubtedly be used. Since this writing is Counter-Economic theory itself, what will be referred to as Counter-Economics is the practice.

Mapping and describing all or even a significantly useful part of Counter-Economics will require at least a full volume itself.[26] Just enough will be sketched here to provide understanding for the rest of the manifesto.

Going from an agorist society to a statist one should be uphill work, equivalent to a path of high negative entropy in physics. After all, once one is living in and understanding a well-run free society, why would one wish to return to systematic coercion, plunder, and anxiety? Spreading ignorance and irrationality among the knowledgeable and rational is difficult; mystifying that which is already clearly understood is nearly impossible. The agorist society should be fairly stable relative to decadence, though highly open to improvement.

Let us run backward in time, like running a film in reverse, from the agorist society to the present statist society. What would we expect to see?

Pockets of statism—mostly contiguous in territory, since the State requires regional

---

[26] This volume, *Counter-Economics* (the book), is in process and will soon be completed, Market willing!

Note to the Fourth Edition: SEK3 died before completing his *magnum opus*, but KoPubCo is in the process of preparing what exists of his manuscript for publication in the near future.

monopolies—would first appear. The remaining victims are becoming more and more aware of the wonderful free world around them and "evaporating" from these pockets. Large syndicates of market protection agencies are containing the State by defending those who have signed up for protection-insurance. Most important, those outside the statist pockets or sub-societies are enjoying an agorist society save for a higher cost of insurance premiums and some care as to where they travel. The agorists could coexist with statists at this point, maintaining an isolationist "foreign policy" since the costs of invasion and liberation of statist sub-societies would be higher than immediate returns (unless the State launches an all-out last aggression). There is, however, no real reason to imagine that the remaining victims will choose to remain oppressed when the libertarian alternative is so visible and accessible. The State's areas are like a supersaturated solution ready to precipitate anarchy.

Run backward another step and we find the situation reversed. We find larger sectors of society under Statism and smaller ones living as agorically as possible. However, there is one visible difference: the agorists need not be territorially contiguous. They can live anywhere, though they will *tend to* associate with their fellow agorists not only for social reinforcement but for ease and profitability of trade. It's always safer and more profitable to deal with more trustworthy customers and suppliers. The tendency is for greater association among more agorist individuals and for dissociation with more statist elements. (This tendency is not only theoretically strong; it already exists in embryonic practice today.) Some easily defendable territories, perhaps in space or islands in the ocean (or under the ocean) or big-city "ghettoes" may be almost entirely agorist, where the State is impotent to crush them. Most agorists, though, will live within statist-claimed areas.

There will be a spectrum of the degree of agorism in most individuals, as there is today, with a few benefiting from the State being highly statist, a few fully conscious of the agorist alternative and competent at living free to the hilt, and the rest in the middle with varying degrees of confusion.

Finally, we step back to where there exist only a handful who understand agorism, the vast majority perceiving illusory gains from the existence of the State or unable to perceive an alternative, and the statists themselves: the government apparatus and the class defined by receiving a net gain from the State's intervention in the Market.[27]

This is a description of our present society. We are "home."

Before we reverse course and describe the path from statism to agorism, let us look around at our present society with our newly acquired agorist perception. Much as a traveler who returns home and sees things in a new light from what he or she has learned from

---

[27] That class has been called the Ruling Class, Power Elite, or Conspiracy, depending on whether the analysis comes from a Marxist, Liberal, or Bircher background. The terms will be used interchangeably to show the commonality of the identification.

foreign lands and ways of life, we may gain new insights on our present circumstances.

Besides a few enlightened New Libertarians tolerated in the more liberal statist areas of the globe ("toleration" exists to the degree of libertarian contamination of statism), we now perceive something else: large numbers on people who are acting in an agorist manner with little understanding of any theory but who are induced by material gain to evade, avoid, or defy the State. Surely they have potential?

In the Soviet Union, a bastion of arch-statism and a nearly totally collapsed "official" economy, a giant black market provides the Russian, Armenian, Ukrainian, and others with everything from food to television repair to official papers and favors from the ruling class. As the *Manchester Guardian Weekly* reports, Burma is almost a total black market with the government reduced to an army, police, and a few strutting politicians. In varying degrees, this is true of nearly all the Second and Third Worlds.

What of the "First" World? In the social-democrat countries, the black market is smaller because the "white market" of legally accepted market transactions is larger, but the former is still quite prominent. Italy, for example, has a "problem" of a large part of its civil service (which works officially from 7 a.m. to 2 p.m.) working unofficially at various jobs the rest of the day to earn "black" money. The Netherlands has a large black market in housing because of the high regulation of this industry. Denmark has a tax evasion movement so large that those in it seduced to politics have formed the second largest party. And these are only the grossest examples that the press has been able or willing to cover. Currency controls are evaded rampantly; in France, for example, everyone is assumed to have a large gold stash and trips to Switzerland for more than touring and skiing are commonplace.

To appreciate fully the extent of this counter-economic activity, one must view the relatively free "capitalist" economies. Let us look at the black and grey markets[28] in North America and remember that this is the case of lowest activity in the world today.

---

[28] While some coercive acts, such as murder and theft, are often lumped into the label "black market," the vast majority of this "organized crime" is perfectly legitimate to a libertarian, though occasionally unsavory. The Mafia, for example, is not black market but a *government* over some of the black market that collects protection money (taxes) from its victims and enforces its control with executions and beatings (law enforcement), and even conducts wars when its monopoly is threatened. These acts will be considered *red market* to differentiate them from the moral acts of the black market, which will be discussed below. In short, the "black market" is anything nonviolent that is prohibited by the State and carried on anyway.

The "grey market" is used here to mean dealing in goods and services not themselves illegal but obtained or distributed in ways legislated against by the State. Much of what is called "white-collar crime" falls under this heading and is smiled upon by most of society.

Where one draws the line between black and grey market depends largely on the state of consciousness of the society in which one lives. The red market is clearly separable: murder is red market. When the State forbids self-defense, defending oneself against a criminal—including a police officer—is black in New York City and grey in Orange County, California.

According to the American Internal Revenue Service, at least twenty million people belong to the "underground economy" of tax evaders using cash or barter exchange to avoid detections of transactions. Millions keep money in gold or in foreign accounts to avoid the hidden taxation of inflation. Millions of "illegal aliens" are employed, according to the Immigration and Naturalization service. Millions more deal or consume marijuana, cocaine, and other proscribed drugs, including laetrile, tryptophan, anti-AIDS drugs, and other forbidden medical material.

And there are all the practitioners of "victimless crimes." Besides drug use, there is prostitution, pornography, bootlegging, false identification papers, gambling, and proscribed sexual conduct between consenting adults. Regardless of "reform movements" to gain political acceptance of these acts, the populace has chosen to *act now*—and by doing so are creating a counter-economy.

It doesn't stop here, though. Since the 55 mph speed limit was enacted federally in the U.S., most Americans have become counter-economic drivers. The trucking industry has developed CB communications to evade State enforcement of regulations. For independents who can make four runs at 75 mph rather than three runs at 55 mph, counter-economic driving is a question of survival.

The ancient custom of smuggling thrives today, from boatloads of marijuana and foreign appliances with high tariffs and truckloads of people from less-developed countries, to the tourists stashing a little extra in their luggage and not reporting it to customs agents.

Nearly everyone engages in some sort of misrepresentation or misdirection on their tax forms, off-the-books payments for services, unreported trade with relatives, and illegal sexual positions with their mates.

To some extent, then, everybody is a counter-economist! And this is predictable from libertarian theory. Nearly every aspect of human action has statist legislation prohibiting, regulating, or controlling it. These laws are so numerous that a "Libertarian" Party that prevented any new legislation and briskly repealed ten or twenty laws a session would not have significantly repealed the State (let alone the mechanism itself!) for millennia![29]

Obviously, the State is unable to obtain enforcement of its edicts. Yet the State continues. And if everyone is somewhat counter-economic, why hasn't the Counter-Economy overwhelmed the economy?

Outside of North America we can add the effect of imperialism. The Soviet Union has received support from the more-developed countries in the 1930s and large quantities of instruments of violence during World War II. Even today, "trade"—heavily subsidized by non-repayable loans—props up the Soviet and now Chinese regimes. This flow of capital (or *anti-capital*, being destructive of value) from both blocs, along with military aid, maintains regimes over the rest of the globe. But that does not explain the North American case.

---

[29] Thus an "L"P would perpetuate statism. In addition, an "L"P would preserve the ill-gotten gain of the ruling class and maintain the State's mechanism of enforcement and execution.

What exists everywhere on Earth that allows the State to continue is the *sanction of the victim.*[30] Every victim of statism has internalized the State to some degree. The IRS's annual proclamation that the income tax depends on "voluntary compliance" is ironically true. Should the taxpayers completely cut off the blood supply, the vampire State would helplessly perish, its unpaid police and army deserting almost immediately, defanging the Monster. If everyone abandoned "legal tender" for gold and goods in contracts and other exchanges, it is doubtful that even taxation could sustain the modern State.[31]

This is where the State's control of education and the information media, either directly or through ruling-class ownership, becomes cru-

---

[30] Thank you, Ayn Rand, for that phrase.

[31] Although this topic is extensively covered in libertarian literature, many are still unaware of the true nature and mechanism of inflation.

Very briefly, a general price rise is only the consequence of inflation, which is the increase of the money supply. Much more damaging is its redistribution of wealth and its side-effects that dislocate the economy. The State "creates" money, which is distributed to the first line of beneficiaries—big bankers, to pay off its warfare/welfare contractors—and to the civil service, the second line of beneficiaries. As they bid up prices with this unbacked purchasing power, everyone else finds themselves unable to buy as much.

The unanticipated rise in price (anticipated inflation is discounted by the market) signals entrepreneurs to invest in capital goods for increased demand. As consumption is cut back because of a lowering of general purchasing power, those entrepreneurs find that they have over-invested and must sell at a loss, lay off employees, and liquidate capital—a depression results. The

cial. In earlier days, the established priesthood served the function to sanctify the king and the aristocracy, to mystify the relations of oppression, and to induce guilt in evaders and resisters. The disestablishment of religion has put this burden on the new intellectual class (what the Russians called the *intelligentsia*). Some intellectuals, holding truth as their highest value (as did earlier dissenting theologians and clerics), do work at clarifying rather than mystifying, but they are dismissed or reviled and kept away from State and foundation-controlled income. Thus is the phenomenon of dissidence and revisionism created; and thus is the attitude of anti-intellectualism generated among the populace, who suspect or incompletely understand the function of the Court Intellectual.

State is often induced by the clamor of unemployed workers and near-bankrupt capitalists to increase the currency supply again to "stimulate" the economy; that is, to create another illusory boom.

Unfortunately, this new injection of inflation must be unanticipated to work; hence, an even larger inflation must ensue. The cycle, if it continues, would lead to runaway inflation (Germany, 1923, is a classic example) and collapse of the currency ("Crack-Up Boom" is Mises's descriptive phrase).

Allegedly free-market economists urge the State to "take the bitter pill" of depression (like an addict going "cold turkey" lest he overdose) to work out the effects of the money injection and cure the system. As can be seen, this is profoundly conservative in maintaining statism.

A far better solution would be for people to abandon State fiat money in favor of uninflatable media of exchange such as gold, silver, commodities, or harder foreign currencies in order to hasten the collapse.

Note well how anarchist intellectuals are attacked and repressed under every State; and those arguing for an overthrow of the present ruling class—even only to replace it with another—are suppressed. Those who propose changes that eliminate some beneficiaries of the State and add others are often lauded by the benefiting elements of the Higher circles and attacked by the potential losers.

A common characteristic of most hardened black marketeers is their guilt. They wish to "make their bundle" and return to the "straight society." Bootleggers and hookers all long someday for reacceptance in society—even when they form a supportive "subsociety" of outcasts. Yet there have been exceptions to this phenomenon of longing for acceptance: the religious dissenting communities of the 1700s, the political utopian communities of the 1800s, and most recently the counter-culture of the hippies and the New Left. What they had was a conviction that their subsociety was superior to the rest of society. The fearful reaction they generated in the rest of society was the fear that they were correct.

All of these examples of self-sustaining subsocieties failed for one overriding reason: ignorance of economics. No social binding, no matter how beautiful, can overcome the basic glue of society—division of labor. The anti-market commune defies the only enforceable law—the law of nature. The basic organizational structure of society (above the family) is not the *commune* (or tribe or extended tribe or State) but the *agora*. No matter how many wish communism to work and devote themselves to it, it will fail. They can hold back agorism indefinitely by great effort, but when they let go, the "flow" or "Invisible Hand" or "tides of history" or "profit incentive" or "doing what comes naturally" or "spontaneity" will carry society inexorably closer to the pure agora.

Why is there such resistance to eventual happiness? Psychologists have been dealing with that since they began their embryonic science. We can at least give two broad answers when it comes to socioeconomic questions: internalization of anti-principles (those that seem to be principles but are actually contrary to natural law) and the opposition of vested interests.

Now we can see clearly what is needed to create a libertarian society. On the one hand we need the education of the libertarian activists and the consciousness-raising of counter-economists to libertarian understanding and mutual supportiveness. "We are right, we are better, we are surviving in a moral, consistent way, *and* we are building a better society—of benefit to ourselves *and* others," our counter-economic "encounter groups" might affirm.

Note well that libertarian activists who are not themselves full practicing counter-economists are unlikely to be convincing. "Libertarian" political candidates undercut everything they say (of value) by what they are doing; some candidates have even held jobs in tax bureaus and defense departments!

On the other hand, we must defend ourselves against the vested interests or at the very least lower their oppression as much as possible. If we eschew reformist activity as counterproductive, how will we achieve that result?

One way is to bring more and more people into the counter-economy and lower the plunder available to the State. But evasion isn't enough; how do we protect ourselves and even counterattack?

Slowly but steadily we will move to the free society, turning more counter-economists on to libertarianism and more libertarians on to counter-economics, finally integrating theory and practice. The counter-economy will grow and spread to the next step we saw in our trip backward, with an ever-larger agorist subsociety imbedded in the statist society. Some agorists may even condense into discernible districts and ghettoes or predominate on islands or in space colonies. At this point, the question of protection and defence will become important.

Using our agorist model (Chapter II), we can see how the protection industry must evolve. First, why do people engage in counter-economics with *no* protection? The payoff for the risk they take is greater than their expected loss. This statement is true, of course, for *all* economic activity, but for counter-economics it requires special emphasis:

The fundamental principle of counter-economics is to trade risk for profit.[32]

---

[32] An example of how this works may be helpful. Suppose I wished to receive and sell contraband or evade a tax or violate a regulation. Let's say I can make $100,000 per transaction.

Using government figures on criminal apprehension—always exaggerated in the State's favor simply because they cannot *know* how much the counter-

The higher the expected profit, the greater the risk taken. Note that if risk is lowered, a lot more would be attempted and accomplished—surely an indicator that a free society is wealthier than an unfree one.

Risk may be lowered by increasing care, taking precautions, tightening security (locks, stashes, safe houses), and by trusting fewer persons of higher trustworthiness. The last indicates a high preference for dealing with fellow agorists and a strong economic incentive that binds an agorist subsociety and provides an incentive to recruit or support recruitment into that subsociety.

---

economy gets away with—I find an apprehension rate of 20%. One may then find out the percentage of those cases that come to trial and the percentage of those that result in a conviction even with a good lawyer. Let's say 25% make it to trial and 50% result in conviction. (The latter is high, but we'll throw in the legal fees involved so that even a decision involving loss of legal costs but acquittal is still a "loss.") I therefore incur a 2.5% risk (.20 x .25 x .50 = 0.025). This is *high* for most real cases.

Suppose my maximum fine is $500,000 or five years in jail—or both. Excluding my counter-economic transactions (one certainly cannot count them when deciding whether or not to do them), I might make $20,000 a year so that I would lose another $100,000 while imprisoned. It's very hard to assign a value to five years of incarceration, but at least in our present society it's not too much worse than other institutionalization (school, army, hospital) and at least the counter-economist won't be plagued with guilt and remorse.

So I weigh 2.5% of $600,000 ($15,000) loss and five years against $100,000 gain! And I could easily insure myself for $15,000 (or less) to pay all costs and fines! In short, it works.

Counter-economic entrepreneurs have an incentive to provide better security devices, places of concealment, instructions to aid evasion and to screen potential customers and suppliers for other counter-economic entrepreneurs. And thus is the counter-economic protection industry born.

As it grows, it may begin insuring against "busts," lowering counter-economic risks further and accelerating counter-economic growth. Then it may provide lookouts and guarded areas of safekeeping with alarm systems and high-tech concealment mechanisms. Guards may be provided against real criminals (other than the State). Already many residential, business, and even minority districts employ private patrols, having given up on the State's alleged protection of property.

Along the way, the risk of contract-violation between counter-economic traders will be lowered by arbitration. Then the protection agencies will start providing contract enforcement between agorists, although the greatest "enforcer" in the early stages will be the State to which each one can betray the other. Yet that act would quickly result in one's expulsion from the subsociety; so an internal enforcement mechanism will be valued.

In the final stages, counter-economist transactions with statists will be enforceable by the protection agencies and the agorists thus protected against the criminality of the State.[33]

---

[33] It probably should be noted explicitly that businesses could grow quite large in the counter-economy. Whether or not "wage workers" would exist instead of "independent contractors" for all steps of production is ar-

At this point we have reached the final step before the achievement of a libertarian society. Society is divided between large, inviolate agorist areas and rapidly shrinking statist sectors.

We stand on the brink of Revolution.

---

guable, but this author feels that the whole concept of "worker/boss" is a holdover from feudalism and not, as Marx claims, fundamental to "capitalism." Of course, capital-statism is the opposite of what the libertarian advocates.

Furthermore, even large businesses today could go partially counter-economic, leaving a portion in the "white market" to satisfy government agents and pay some modicum of taxes and report a token number of workers. The rest of the business would (and already often does) expand off the books with independent contractors who supply, service, and distribute the finished product. Nobody, no business, no worker, and no entrepreneur *need* be white market.

IV. Revolution: Our Strategy

Our condition has been analyzed, our goal perceived, the mechanism has been spelled out and a set of pathways have been mapped out. Should we simply go counter-economic ourselves, educate ourselves in libertarianism, and inform others by word and deed, we shall reach our libertarian society. Indeed, this is sufficient for most people and enough to be expected. No New Libertarian should ever berate libertarian counter-economists for not doing more. They are agorists and will get there in their own time.

Even these simple agorists, though, may wish to contribute to entrepreneurs who specialize in accelerating the movement toward the agorist society and away from statism. And others, perceiving rising inflation heading toward economic collapse or the gathering clouds of war, will want something *done* about it. Finally, the counterattacks of the State that subvert the agorist subsociety and lure libertarians into false paths must be combated. These tasks define the field for the New Libertarian activist.[34]

Again—for those who wish only to live their lives as freely as possible and associate with

[34] Many agorists such as Pyro Egon have challenged the New Libertarians on this point. As far as they are concerned, the manifesto this far is the entire program and any further "activism" is "movementism" and leads one ineluctably back toward statism.

others like-minded—counter-economic libertarianism is sufficient. No more is needed.

For those, however, who want to support in whatever way they can those heroic entrepreneurs who specialize in recruiting for the agora, deal with state-caused catastrophes, and combat statists within and without, a guide is needed to select out those who are "doing something worthwhile" from those who are spinning their wheels and those who are actually counterproductive (i.e., counterrevolutionary). And for those, like this author, who burn for Liberty and wish to devote themselves to that life's work, a strategy is essential. What follows, then, is the New Libertarian Strategy.[35]

The New Libertarian activist must keep in mind that actual defense against the State is impossible until the counter-economy has generated syndicates of protection agencies sufficiently large to defend against the remnant of the State. This will occur only at the "phase transition" between the third and fourth steps leading back from our statism to agorism (Chapter III).

Each step from statism to agorism requires a different strategy; tactics will differ even within each step. There are *some* rules that will apply in all stages.

Under all circumstances, one recruits and educates. Given typically confused individual acquaintances who consider a counter-economic act, encourage them to do it. If they are intelligent enough and not likely to turn on you, explain risks involved and return ex-

---

[35] *New Libertarian Strategy* is the newsletter of the Movement of the Libertarian Left—not coincidentally.

pected. Most of all, educate them by *your* example to the extent you can let them know.

All "Library Libertarians" you know—those who profess some theoretical variant of libertarianism but eschew its practice—should be encouraged to practice what they preach. Scorn their inaction, praise their first halting steps toward counter-economics. Interact with them more and more as trust grows with their competence and experience.

Those already in counter-economics whom you meet can be "let in on" the libertarian philosophy that you hold, that mysterious belief you possess that keeps you so happy and free of guilt. Drop it nonchalantly if they feign lack of interest; wax enthusiastic as they grow more curious and eager to learn.

Sell agorism by example and argument. Control and program your emotional reactions to exhibit hostility at statism and deviationism, and to exhibit enthusiasm and joy at agorist acts and the State's setbacks. Most of these tactics will come with routine, but you can check yourself to polish a few things.

Finally, coordinate your activities with other New Libertarian activists. At this point, we arrive at the need for group tactics and organization.

Many worthy libertarians argue that the market structures of businesses, partnerships, and joint-stock companies[36] provide all the organiza-

[36] But not a "corporation", which is a fictitious "individual" created by the State and endowed with privileges. Some privileges besides subsidies and tariffs are special tax rates, limited liability, legal benefits in court disputes, licenses, and exemption from regulation. True, they have some drawbacks but none compared to an unincorporated white-market business.

tion necessary or desirable; save maybe for personal mating or socializing. In one sense they are correct in that all structures must be market-compatible or be inconsistent with agorism. In another sense, they are guilty of a lack of imagination and a concern for form over substance.

In an agorist society, division of labor and self-respect of each worker-capitalist-entrepreneur will probably eliminate the traditional business organization—especially the corporate hierarchy, an imitation of the State and not the Market. Most companies will be associations of independent contractors, consultants, and other companies. Many may be just one entrepreneur and all his services, computers, suppliers, and customers. This mode of operation is already around and growing in the freer segments of western economies.

Thus an association of entrepreneurs of liberty for the purpose of specializing, co-ordinating, and delivering libertarian activities is no violation of the market and may well be optimal. The traditional name for a banding together of sovereign units for a goal and then disbanding is an *alliance*. Hence the basic organization for New Libertarian activists is the *New Libertarian Alliance*.[37]

[37] The first New Libertarian Alliance was formed, prematurely in many respects, by this author in 1974 from recruits from a raid on the "L"P, from other movement activists, and from a few counter-economists. The market proved less than ready for a growth in this business and so the NLA to date has spent most of its energies toward building that market.

Any New Libertarians can call themselves a New Libertarian Alliance without "official authorization"; most may wish to coordinate themselves with other NLA groups and seek common strategy, though tactics may differ due to different conditions of the Allies.

The organization of NLA (or NLAs) is simple and should avoid turning into a political organ or even an authoritarian organization. Rather than officers, what are needed are tacticians (local coordinators with competency in tactical planning) and strategists (regional coordinators with competency in strategic thinking). A New Libertarian Ally does not *follow* a tactician or strategist but rather "buys" their argument and expertise. Anyone offering a better plan can replace the previous planner. Tactics and strategy should be "bought and sold" by the Allies like any other commodity in consistent agorist fashion.

Even though these labels are borrowed from military history and do correspond to a form of combat, never forget that actual physical confrontation with the State's enforcers must await the market's generation of protection agency syndicates of sufficient strength; all else is premature.[38]

What is the global strategy, continental strategy, and local tactics for an NLA optimally

---

[38] This mode of NLA organization worked well for the Long Beach chapter that kept it constantly in practice. Regional strategy was not fully "shaken down" by practice but no other NLA group maintained that high a level of committed Allies who were constantly developing and working that theory.

As for armies, it should be noted that Nestor Makhno ran an army in fairly anarchist manner with a small core of officers and complete volunteers filling the ranks when needed or convinced of the need. He fought Reds and Whites successfully in the Ukraine 1918-20 until overwhelmed by weight of numbers of the victorious Red statists combining the full resources of a continent against him.

to pursue? Again, let's look at the four steps from agora from statism (or from statism to agora). The first three are actually rather artificial divisions: no abrupt change occurs from first to second to third. As will be shown, it is most probable that the transition from the third to fourth step will be quite sudden, though it is not required by the nature of the agora; rather, the convulsion will be caused by the nature of the State. In fact, all violence, unrest, instability, and dislocations are caused by the State—never fomented by New Libertarians.

Heed well, you who would be a paladin of Liberty: *never initiate any act of violence regardless of how likely a "libertarian" result may appear*. To do so is to reduce yourself to a statist. There are *no* exceptions to this rule. Either you are fundamentally consistent or you are not. A New Libertarian is fundamentally consistent and one who is not fundamentally consistent is not a New Libertarian.[39]

Using New Libertarian analysis, however, one can predict the likely outbreak of statist

---

[39] No membership or credentials are needed or desirable for the NLA. Of course, one may make a list of those with whom to gather and plan, and to whom to mail communications. But there is nothing sacred or special about such lists; they are merely one strategist or tactician's judgment.

One cannot be purged from NLA. One is either a New Libertarian or not according to the evidence provided by one's acts; other Allies must judge for themselves. All who accept you as a New Libertarian are in Alliance with you; those who reject you are not, though you may be in Alliance with others.

aggression and move to head it off by exposure or even defend or evacuate the victims. One can also predict the probable outcomes of deviations by libertarian groups and either head off the sellouts and disasters or win respect for one's foresight and that of New Libertarianism from potential recruits. Let the State be the forest fire; the NLA are the smoke-eaters who know how it burns, how to fire-break, how the winds of change affect it, where the sparks may fly, and, finally, how to extinguish it.

With this in mind, let us label the steps to agora as four phases and outline the appropriate strategy for each.

PHASE 0: ZERO-DENSITY AGORIST SOCIETY

In this phase—most of human history—no agorists exist, only scattered libertarians or proto-libertarian thinkers and practicing counter-economists. The moment someone reads this manifesto and wishes to apply it, we have moved to the next phase. All that can be done in Phase 0 is slow evolution of consciousness, hit-or-miss development, and a lot of frustrating dichotomies.

Until you—the first agorist in a Phase 0 situation—have added to your number, your only strategy can be to increase your numbers, as well as live counter-economically yourself. The best form of organization is a Libertarian Alliance in which you steer the members from political activity (where they have blindly gone seeking relief from oppression) and focus on education, publicity, recruitment, and perhaps some *anti-political* campaigning (*viz*. "Vote For Nobody," "None of the Above," "Boycott the Ballot," "Don't vote, it only Encourages Them!" *etc*.) to publicize the libertarian alternative. An LA may take stands on issues agreed on, but insist on unanimity. Only the most clearly libertarian stands will be taken and you can always veto a deviationist stance. Always encourage tendencies toward "hard-core" (consistent) positions and scorn "soft-core" (inconsistent) ones.

PHASE 1: LOW-DENSITY AGORIST SOCIETY

The first counter-economic libertarians appear in this phase and the first serious splits in the Libertarian movement occur. Since few libertarians are very consistent yet, deviationism will run rife and tend to overwhelm activism. "Get-Liberty-Quick" schemes from anarchozionism (running away to a Promised Land of Liberty) to political opportunism will seduce the impatient and sway the incompletely informed. All will fail if for no other reason than that Liberty grows individual by individual. *Mass conversion is impossible.* There is one exception—radicalization caused by statist attack against a collective. Even so, it requires entrepreneurs of Liberty to have sufficiently informed the persecuted collective so that they *lase* coherently libertarian-ward rather than scatter randomly or, worse, flow into out-of-power statism. These Crises of Statism are spontaneous *and* predictable—but cannot be *caused* by moral, consistent libertarians.

The strategy of the first New Libertarians is to combat the anti-principles that strengthen the State and uselessly dissipate anarchist energy. The general strategy outlined previously applies: get libertarians into counter-economics and persuade the most active of the agorists to get counter-economists into libertarianism.

The proto-New Libertarians may work within existing organizations and clubs of Libertarians as "radical caucuses," ginger groups, or as a "Libertarian Left" faction in general. An NLA is premature here because it is not yet self-sustaining.

What can be successfully built is—under whatever label seems most conducive to recruitment—a *Movement of the Libertarian Left*. Such a Movement is itself a mixed bag of individuals of varying "hardness of core" but they are *tending* or *moving* toward the ideal of New Libertarianism. Even within MLL, structure should be de-emphasized. The most New Libertarian will be the most competent to coordinate and plan; that is, those of highest understanding and practice of agorism *and* greatest zeal for action will naturally direct resources. Each MLLer, like each NL Ally, spends his or her own resources and decides whether or not to accept a tactician's or strategist's advice and planning, as any entrepreneur would do with any informed consultant. *Some* pseudo-political public trappings may be necessary to utilize public forums and media access; also, most people will not *understand* your market-organization unless you translate it into pseudo-political terminology and back again.

At this point, in the latter stages of Phase 1 and with a functioning MLL large enough, these hard-core dedicated "cadre" can actually apply leverage to sway larger groups of semi-converted quasi-libertarians to block marginal actions by the State. This is a high-expenditure, "quick gain," but low long-range yield tactic and should be rare. (It will be covered later; basically, stave off war and mass extermination of libertarians.)

Following all these activities, radicalizing the libertarians, and evolving the NLA. That is all one can accomplish.

PHASE 2: MID-DENSITY, SMALL CONDENSATION AGORIST SOCIETY

At this point the statists take notice of agorism. While before libertarians could be manipulated by one ruling faction to the detriment of another (sort of anti-market "competition," played with ballots and bullets rather than innovation and pricing), they will start to be perceived as a threat. Pogroms (mass arrests) may even occur, although that is unlikely. Remember, most agorists are imbedded in the rest of society and associating with them are partially-converted libertarians and counter-economists. In order to reach this phase, the entire society has been contaminated by agorism to a degree. Thus it is now possible for the first "ghettoes" or districts of agorists to appear and count on the sympathy of the rest of society to restrain the State from a mass attack.[40]

These communities, whether above or underground, can now sustain the New Libertarian Alliance. NLA acts as spokesman for the agora within the statist society, using every chance to publicize the superiority of agorist living to statist inhabiting and perhaps argue for tolerance of those with "different ways."[41]

In this phase, the agorist society is vulnerable to statist regression of the populace. Thus the agorists, whether visible or not, have a high incentive at least to maintain the present level of libertarian consciousness among the rest of the populace. This being done

---

[40] Premature appearance of agorist communities will lead to their violent suppression by the State. The NLA must defend those who can be saved when historical conditions are marginal and warn and evacuate those who are doomed.

[41] It is still within the limits of New Libertarian morality to point out to one faction of the Higher Circles that the agorist existence benefits them more than the other faction. While no statist can ever be aided in plunder and murder—and even allying with one statist against another consumes scarce resources for the outcome of merely trading oppressors—the New Libertarian can perceive that simply by existing and conducting usual business, the agorist activity is relatively more detrimental to one group of statists over another.

A good rule of thumb to the tactic of playing off ruling groups is to make sure that no more resources are devoted to it than extra statements based in regular publications and media exposure for more important work ... and in private conversations, if one frequents *those* social circles.

This tactic fails when the agorist society is perceived as too threatening; then all statist factions unite to save their skins.

most expertly by the NLA (one way to define who the NLA *is* at this phase), the NLA has its sustenance and its mission. But in addition to "defending" the agorist subsociety, it can work toward accelerating the next evolutionary step.

PHASE 3: HIGH-DENSITY, LARGE CONDENSATION AGORIST SOCIETY

In this phase, the State moves into a series of terminal crises, somewhat analogous to the well-known Marxist scenario, but with different causes—in this case, real ones. Fortunately, the potential for damage has been drastically reduced by the sapping of the State's resources and the corrosion of its authority by the growth of the Counter-Economy.

In fact, as the resources of the economy approach equality between the State and Agora, the State is *pushed* into crisis. Wars and rampant inflation with depressions and crack-ups become perpetual as the State attempts to redeem its authority. It *may* be possible to reverse its decline by corrupting the agora with seductive anti-principles, so the NLA's first task is clear: to maintain vigilance and purity of thought. In this phase, the NLA may no longer hold either label or much of its old form. The most motivated New Libertarians will move into the research and development segments of the budding agorist protection and arbitration agencies and into positions as directors of the protection company syndicates.

The situation now approaches revolution but is still reversible.[42] Again the New Libertarians are in the forefront of maintaining and defending gains to this point, but are looking ahead to the next phase.

The NLA (now just a collective term for the most forward-looking elements) can accelerate the process by discovering and developing the optimal methods of protection and defense, both by word and deed, for their industry and by entrepreneuring its innovations.

At this phase transition between 3 and 4 we have the last unleashing of violence by the Ruling Class of the State to suppress those elements that would bring them to justice for all past state crimes. The State's intellectuals perceive that its authority has failed and all will be lost; things must be reversed now or never. The NLA must prevent premature awareness of this status *or* premature action on this awareness. This is the final strategic goal of the NLA.

When the State unleashes its final wave of suppression—and is successfully resisted—this is the definition of *Revolution*. Once realization has occurred that the State no longer can plunder and pay off its parasitical class, the enforcers will switch sides to those better able to pay them and the State will rapidly implode into a series of pockets of statism in backward areas—if any.[43]

---

[42] Let's say one region is highly agorist and the rest more primitive. Resources may be transferred by the State to crush this premature and localized (thus vulnerable) agora. This applies to Phase 2 even more.

[43] Some will argue that the State may collapse peacefully when the statists see the end approaching. If statists were so reasonable about not resorting to force because of market alternatives, *they wouldn't be statists*. Revolution is as inevitable as any human action can be.

PHASE 4: AGORIST SOCIETY WITH STATIST IMPURITIES

The collapse of the State leaves only mopping-up operations. Since the insurance and protection companies see no State to defend against, the syndicate of allied protectors collapses into competition and the NLA—its support gone—dissolves. Statists apprehended pay restoration and—if they live long enough to discharge their debts—are re-integrated as productive entrepreneurs. (Their "training" comes automatically as they work off their debt.)

We're home (Chapter II)! New Libertarianism is taken for granted as the basis of ordinary life and we tackle the other problems facing mankind.

V. ACTION! OUR TACTICS

The previous chapter discussed some tactics in passing. A few that have been found productive for radical libertarians and the MLL include infiltration of less-radical groups and sparking splits by presenting alternatives; confrontation of coercion (or deviation) with visible protest and rejection; day-to-day personal salesmanship among friends; libertarian social groups such as supper clubs to exchange information, goods, and support and to act as a proto-agora; and, of course, publication, public speaking, writing fiction with agorist messages[44], and educational activities in many forms: teacher, business consultant, entertainer, revisionist historian, agorist economist, etc.

Successful tactics can only be discovered and used and passed on. Those who perceive sufficiently similar conditions in time and place to those of another where a tactic worked can use it. But it is all a risk; that is what activism is, a type of entrepreneurship, of guessing the market and supplying the demand. One can become better and better at making good guesses; that's what makes a successful entrepreneur. It's all in *Human Action* by Von Mises if you can apply it.

---

[44] *E.g., Alongside Night* by J. Neil Schulman (Crown, 1979: Ace, 1982, Avon 1987, SoftServ, 1990, Pulpless, 1999) and expected sequels.

To find out what has been tried and worked or failed, communication is necessary. If you have reached this page and agreed, and have a desire to support resistance or a burning need to resist coercion, you are ready for the MLL or NLA in existence, depending on the phase we are currently in (Chapter IV). Free yourself. Get active.

What phase are we in? In October 1980, (first edition) most of the planet Earth is in **Phase 0**. The British Isles, Australia, and Canada have moved substantially toward **Phase 1**; North America is in **Phase 1**. Only in the highest concentration of libertarians today, in Southern California, are the first signs of **Phase 2**. Assuming the situation is not reversed, the first few droplets of actual agorist societies—anarchovillages—are nucleating a viable subsociety.

The Movement of the Libertarian Left exists only in California with a few scattered nuclei—agents and cells—in Alliance. The New Libertarian Alliance previously proclaimed was found premature and NLA remains in embryo (or nucleus) until objective conditions arrive to sustain it.

The MLL has its work cut out for it. Externally, the worldwide collapse of the "Left"[45]

[45] The Left was originally proto-Libertarian, as revisionist historians such as Leonard Liggio point out. In the French Assembly, free marketeer Frederic Bastiat sat next to anarchist Pierre-Joseph Proudhon. Even today Marxists refer to anarchists as "ultra-left" elements. The libertarian and Marxist elements were about equal at the close of the First Workingman's International. The Marxists and their sellout imitators have been in ascendancy since the 1890s, finally losing be-

has weakened restraints on the competitive segments of the state who are rushing toward war to remystify their restive victims with patriotism. Seizing the abandoned leadership of the anti-imperialism, anti-war, and anti-conscription movement with a fresh, invigorating, ideological backing has become an opportunity for libertarians to *become* the Left. MLL has to compete with partyarch and monocentrist elements for this preeminence.[46]

The lurching of American plutocracy from the brink of runaway inflation to depression and back again—in ever wilder swings—has panicked large numbers of complacent businessmen and raised their consciousness beyond conservative assurances of restoring stability to consider radical and even revolutionary alternatives. Only the *Libertarian* Left can steer these entrepreneurs toward an "ideological," non-pragmatic position. Therein lie our opportunities.

Internally, the "Libertarian" Party has reached a crisis with the 1980 American Presidential election. The premature unmasking of the statism inherent in partyarchy by Crane-Clark's blatant opportunism has managed to generate not only Left opposition but *Right* and *Center* opposition.[47] Major defections mount

---

lief in themselves with the New Left collapse, the invasion of Czechoslovakia and Afghanistan by the U.S.S.R. and Viet Nam by China—the "impossible" war between two Marxist States.

[46] Currently, "L" P "R" C and SLS respectively.

[47] The "Right" of current libertarianism is fairly principled, but many of the principles hewed to are anti-principles: gradualism, conservatism, reformism, and minarchy. *Reason* magazine and its *Frontlines* news-

daily.[48]

The failure of reformist elements to oust the Kochtopus by the Denver Convention (August 1981) and lull the unradicalized back in line would set the U.S.L.P. back dramatically and generate thousands of disillusioned recruits for the MLL and anti-party educational and counter-economic activities.

With this manifesto as manual and inspiration, New Libertarian strategists and tacticians can research, develop, correct, and enact the New Libertarian Strategy and the tactics appropriate to the conditions met. Much work is needed but the projects have conse-

---

letter are its main organs. The "Center" includes Murray Rothbard and his following, now organized in the LP "Radical" Caucus, which support Clark "critically," i.e., externally, but not internally. The Rothbard Centrists have moved Left by abandoning monocentrism.

[48] Murray Rothbard as mentioned; the Southern California party Council Director, Dyanne Petersen; others informing this writer of their imminent defection should more "selling-out" occur. It will.

Special Note to Second Edition: It did.

A steady trickle of LP defectors have added to the ranks of MLL month by month since then. At least one new Left Libertarian group, the Voluntaryists, have arisen to compete for the ex-partyarchs. And Murray Rothbard is organizing, at this time, a last-ditch showdown for control of the LP with the Kochtopus remnant at the LP presidential nominating convention to be held in September 1983 in New York City.

Special Note to the Third Edition: It persists to this very day.

The LP continues to co-opt idealistic young radicals, suck out their enthusiasm, disillusion them, and either drive them into pessimistic apathy or deliver them—radicalised and re-energised by their disappointment—to the welcoming arms of agorism.

quences no mundane work can provide: an end to politics, to taxation, to conscription, to economic catastrophe, to involuntary poverty, and to the mass murder of warfare in the final war: society against Our Enemy, The State.

Counter-economics provides immediate gratification for those who abandon statist restraint. Libertarianism rewards the practitioner who follows it with more self-liberation and personal fulfillment than any alternative yet conceived. But only New Libertarianism offers reformation of society into a moral, working way of life without changing the nature of Man. Utopias may be discarded; at last we have a glimpse of how to remold society to fit Man rather than Man to fit some society. What more rewarding challenge could be offered?

Should you now have chosen the New Libertarian path, you may wish to join us in our "Triple A" oath and battle cry—or something similar—and renew yourself with it regularly:

> "We witness to the efficacy of freedom and exult in the intricate beauty of complex voluntary exchange. We demand the right of *every* ego to maximize its value without limit save that of another ego. We proclaim the age of the Market unbound, the natural and proper condition for humanity, wealth in abundance, goals without end or limit, and self-determined meaning for all: *Agora*.
>
> "We challenge all who would bind us to show cause; failing proof of our aggression we shatter our fetters. We bring to justice all who have aggressed against

any, ever. We restore all who have suffered oppression to their rightful condition. And we destroy forever the Monster of the Ages, the pseudo-legitimized monopoly of coercion, from our minds and from our society, the protector of aggressors and thwarter of justice. That is, we smash the State: *Anarchy*.

"We exert our wills to our personal limits, restrained only by consistent morality. We struggle against anti-principles that would sap our wills and combat all who physically challenge us. We rest not nor waste resource until the State is smashed and humanity has reached its agorist home. Burning with unflagging desire for Justice now and Liberty forever, we win: *Action!*

"Agora. Anarchy. *Action!*"

—Samuel Edward Konkin III
October 12, 1980
AnarchoVillage (Long Beach)

Critiques of *New Libertarian Manifesto* by Murray N. Rothbard, Ph.D. Robert LeFevre & Erwin S. Strauss

With Replies by the Author of *New Libertarian Manifesto*

Samuel Edward Konkin III

as originally published in

Strategy of the New Libertarian Alliance

Number One
May Day 1981

INTRODUCTION BY SAMUEL EDWARD KONKIN III CONTINENTAL STRATEGIST — NLA

Libertarianism is, perhaps, too diverse and pluralist to produce the kinds of journals abounding on Left and Right with a fully specified theoretical framework, adjusting as empirical evidence warrants, but mainly analyzing events and competing ideologies for the purpose of mapping out a strategy for the activist, cadre, cell member, or entrepreneur. Libertarianism says too little (albeit correctly) about too many. It defines who are accepted in the society (and who are not) but not who are *making that society* and who effectively oppose it.

New Libertarianism applies a lens—narrowing (and, to anticipate criticism, even distorting)—but *focusing*. And many libertarian activists have felt that need for focus in recent years and have sensed the pull of false paths they *know* will lead not to Liberty but to Power, yet which do provide focus and direction.

New Libertarian Manifesto was the first document to take libertarianism as a given and develop a strategy that it claimed derived from the constraints and insights of libertarianism. As such it contained the weakness of not having earlier, failed examples to build on and refine from.

With that in mind, the Nucleus of the New Libertarian Alliance requested criticism from the major poles of libertarian thought, hoping that the crossfire would weed out the errors and shake down the framework. The poles, as the author sees it, are most ably represented by Murray Rothbard, Robert LeFevre, Roy Childs, Robert Poole, "Filthy Pierre" [or Erwin S. Strauss] (of the *Libertarian Connection*), and Andrew J. Galambos. All of these are poles or nuclei of orbits of thought and generally accepted as fairly distinct.

Galambos refuses to talk to anyone else in the movement, so it was no surprise to receive his non-recognition. Significantly, that *is* the appropriate Galambosian response and so we have it. Childs, the court intellectual of the Charles Koch-owned faction of anarchocentrists, refused to reply directly but sent back second-hand dark mutterings of an unforgotten slight he had received from *NLM*'s author years ago in *New Libertarian Weekly*. Putting personality over principle is the response of the "Kochtopus," then, and is accepted as *their* apt reply to *NLM*.

Poole actually replied to an invitation to criticize *NLM* and said he'd find someone around the office who might want to do it. The *Reason* bureaucracy failed to disgorge anything by press time (after several months' warning), and, one supposes, that is *their* appropriate response to *NLM*.

Fortunately, the "top of the Movement" did reply. Murray N. Rothbard proved again that neither is he too elevated to stoop to principle, nor, as he indicated by his first footnote, would he let even personal affronts deter him. The same spirit and ideological nobility is deemable to Robert LeFevre. Filthy Pierre, like the author himself, has a good fannish mentality about "loccing" other publications.

The critiques of *New Libertarian Manifesto* are printed in full; the responses are not. Something had to give in the space requirements. Nonetheless, the Nucleus of the NLA views *NLM* as well-defended and, next issue, we will move to the attack.

Internal New Libertarian criticism and external criticism will never be closed. So to continue the debate, if others wish, *SNLA* will inaugurate a *Letters* column (in smaller type if it gets out of hand) next issue. Write freely!

And next issue, *Strategy of the New Libertarian Alliance #2*, Samuel Edward Konkin III and other libertarian and agorist theorists (now being solicited) will tackle *Marxism* and especially the Leninist model of Revolution and contrast it with the New Libertarian Revolutionary model (*NL* will try to get a worthy representative of a purist "Left Communist" group to participate.)

It's too early to guarantee *SNLA3* yet*, but undoubtedly it will carry responses to the publication of Konkin's mass-market followup to *NLM*; that is, *Counter-Economics*, the book. And further incursions into the frontier...

---

*Indeed, none was ever produced prior to SEK3's death in 2004. —VK

KONKIN ON LIBERTARIAN STRATEGY BY MURRAY N. ROTHBARD, PH.D.

It is good to have *New Libertarian Manifesto* in more or less systematic form for assessment and criticism. Until now, the Konkinian vision has only been expressed in scattered potshots at his opponents, often me.* It turns out that Sam Konkin's situation is in many ways like the Marxists. Just as the Marxists are far more cogent in their criticisms of existing society than in setting forth their vaporous and rather absurd vision of the communist future, so Konkin is far more coherent in his criticisms of the existing libertarian movement than in outlining his own positive agoric vision. This of course is not an accident. For one thing, it is far easier to discover flaws in existing institutions than to offer a cogent alternative, and secondly it is tactically more comfortable to be on the attack.

---

* One of his criticisms (page 20, footnote 12) is untrue as well as insulting. Neither I nor the *Libertarian Forum* was ever in any sense "bought" or "bought out" by Charles Koch. The *Libertarian Forum* has never had a penny from outside sources; since its inception, it has been entirely self-financing. And while my two year leave at the Cato Institute was enjoyable in many ways, I lost rather than made money by the deal.

I. THE KONKINIAN ALTERNATIVE

In this particular case, Konkin is trying to cope with the challenge I laid down years ago to the anti-party libertarians: O.K., what is *your* strategy for the victory of liberty? I believe Konkin's agorism to be a total failure, but at least he has tried, which is to his credit, and puts him in a class ahead of his anti-party confreres, who usually fall back on fasting, prayer, or each one finding ways to become a better and more peaceful person, none of which even begins to answer the problem of State power and what to do about it. So before I comment on Konkin's criticisms of current libertarian institutions, I would like to take up his agoric alternative.

First, there is a fatal flaw which not only vitiates Konkin's agoric strategy but also permits him to evade the whole problem of organization (see below). This is Konkin's astonishing view that working for wages is somehow non-market or anti-libertarian, and would disappear in a free society. Konkin claims to be an Austrian free-market economist, and how he can say that a voluntary sale of one's labor for money is somehow illegitimate or unlibertarian passeth understanding. Furthermore, it is simply absurd for him to think that in the free market of the future, wage-labor will disappear. Independent contracting, as lovable as some might see it, is simply grossly uneconomic for manufacturing activity. The transactions costs would be far too high. It is absurd, for example, to think of automobile manufacturing conducted by self-employed independent contractors. Furthermore, Konkin is clearly unfamiliar with the fact that the emergence of wage-labor was an enormous boon for many thousands of poor workers and saved them from starvation. If there is no wage labor, as there was not in most production before the Industrial Revolution, then each worker must have enough money to purchase his own capital equipment and tools. One of the great things about the emergence of the factory system and wage labor is that poor workers did not have to purchase their own capital equipment; this could be left to the capitalists. (Thus, see F.A. Hayek's brilliant "Introduction" in his *Capitalism and the Historians.*)

Konkin's fallacious and unlibertarian rejection of wage-labor, however, allows him to do several things. It allows him to present a wildly optimistic view of the potential scope of the black market. It also accounts for his curious neglect of the "white market," and his dismissal of it as unimportant. In point of fact, even though the black market is indeed important in Russia, Italy, etc., it is enormously dwarfed in importance by the legal, white market. So the Konkinian vision of black-market institutions growing, defending themselves and thus *becoming* the free-market anarchist society of the future collapses on this ground alone. Note that black markets are concentrated either in service industries or in commodities, which are both valuable and easily concealed: jewels, gold, drugs, candy bars, stockings, *etc.* This is all well and good, but it still does not solve the problem: who will make automobiles, steel, cement, *etc.* How would *they* fare in the black market? The answer is that they don't fare at all, just as they don't fare in the independent contracting agora.

The point is that these fatal gaps in the Konkinian vision are linked together. By concentrating on such objects as marijuana as his paradigm of the agora, rather than automobiles, steel, Wonder Bread, or whatever, Konkin is able to neglect the overwhelming bulk of economic life and to concentrate on marginalia. Only by this sort of neglect can he even begin to postulate a world of independent contractors or a world of black markets.

And there is another vital point here too. Konkin's entire theory speaks only to the interests and concerns of the marginal classes who are self-employed. The great bulk of the people are full-time wage-workers; they are people with steady jobs. Konkinism has nothing whatsoever to say to these people. To adopt Konkin's strategy, then, would on this ground alone, serve up a dead end for the libertarian movement. We cannot win if there is no possibility of speaking to the concerns of the great bulk of wage-earners in this and other countries.

It is the same thing with tax rebellion, which presumably serves as part of the agorist strategy. For once again, it is far easier for someone who doesn't earn a wage to escape the reporting of his income. It is almost impossible for wage-earners, whose taxes are of course deducted off the top by the infamous withholding tax. Once again, it is impossible to convert wage-workers to the idea of non-payment of taxes because they literally have no choice. Konkin's airy dismissal of taxation as being in some sense voluntary again ignores the plight of the wage-earner.

I am afraid, indeed, that there is only one way to eliminate the monstrous withholding tax. Dare I speak its name? It is *political action*.

It is no accident, again, that the entire spectrum of the black market movement, from tax rebels to agorist theoreticians, are almost exclusively self-employed. To echo Konkin's distinction, black marketeers might well benefit themselves in the *micro* sense, but they have no relevance to the "macro" struggle for liberty and against the State. Indeed, in a kind of reverse invisible hand, they might even be counterproductive. It is possible that the Soviet black market, for example, is so productive that it keeps the entire monstrous Soviet regime afloat, and that without it the Soviet system would collapse. This does not mean, of course, that I scorn or oppose black market activities in Russia; it is just to reveal some of the unpleasant features of the real world.

There are other problems with the agoric concept. I tend to side with Mr. Pyro Egon in his dispute with Konkin; for the black market, if it develops at all, is going to develop on its own, and I see no role whatever for Mr. Konkin and the New Libertarian Alliance or the Movement of the Libertarian Left. Konkin speaks correctly of the division of labor. Well, nowhere does the division of labor manifest itself more clearly than in who succeeds in entrepreneurship. If the black market should develop, then the successful entrepreneurs are not going to be agoric theoreticians like Mr. Konkin but successful entrepreneurs period.

What do they need with Konkin and his group? I suggest, nothing at all. There is a hint in *NLM* that libertarians would *a priori* make better entrepreneurs than anyone else because they are more trustworthy and more rational, but this piece of nonsense was exploded by hard experience a long time ago. Neither do the budding black marketeers need Mr. Konkin and his colleagues to cheer them on and free them of guilt. Again, experience has shown that they do fine on their own, and that urging them on to black market activities is like exhorting ducks to swim.

When we consider, then, the vital importance of wage-work, black markets are already severely limited, and the agorist scenario for the ultimate libertarian goal falls apart. And then there is the final stage where black market agencies use force to defend illegal transactions, tax rebels, *etc.* against the State. Although Konkin doesn't acknowledge it as such, this is violent revolution, and it is simply an historical truth without exception that no violent revolution has come close to succeeding in a democratic country with free elections. So that way is barred too. And it hasn't succeeded all that often even in a dictatorship. The Soviet system has now been oppressing its citizens for over sixty years; and there has been a widespread black market all this time. And yet there is still the Gulag. Why hasn't the black market developed into a Konkinian agora or even hinted at such?

No. Much as I love the market, I refuse to believe that when I engage in a regular market transaction (*e.g.*, buying a sandwich) or a black market activity (*e.g.* driving at 60 miles per hour) I advance one iota nearer the libertarian revolution The black market is not going to be the path to liberty, and libertarian theoreticians and activists have no function in that market. I think this is why the only *real* activity of Mr. Konkin and his colleagues is confined to annoying members of the Libertarian Party. This hectoring may be bracing for the soul of some party members, but it scarcely serves to satisfy the lifelong commitment the Konkinians have to the cause of liberty. No, agorism is a dead end, and, to use an old Stalinist term, is "objectively counterrevolutionary."

II. THE PROBLEM OF ORGANIZATION

I turn now to Konkin's critique of the current libertarian movement, in *NLM* and other writings. There are three basic threads in this critique which are entirely distinct, but which Konkin generally confuses and conflates. These are: the problem of hierarchical organization, the problem of the "Kochtopus," and the Libertarian Party. Generally, Konkin lumps them all together, and thereby confuses all these issues. We must unpack them. Let us do so by first assuming, for the sake of argument, that there is no Libertarian Party, and that there are simply other libertarian institutions, organizations, institutes, magazines, or whatever.

Would Konkin's complaints disappear if the LP collapsed? Clearly not. For there runs through his writings an attack, not only on hierarchical organization but on organization *per se*. He is against joint stock companies because they are organized hierarchically, and seems to be against all other voluntary organizations for similar reasons. He not only opposes wages, he also wants only individual alliances, and not organizations at all.

First, there is nothing either un-libertarian or un-market about a voluntary organization, whether joint-stock or any other. People organize because they believe they can accomplish things more effectively that way than through independent contracting or *ad hoc* alliances. And so they can. So, 1) they are not immoral or unlibertarian and 2) they are the only way by which almost anything can be accomplished, whether it is making automobiles or setting up bridge or chess tournaments. Konkin's suggested floating affinity groups can accomplish very little, and *that* when only a handful of people are involved. But if more than a handful wish to cooperate on joint tasks, whether steel-making or chess tournaments, an organization becomes necessary.

Organizations, of course, create problems, and it is really pointless to go on about them. If more than three or four people wish to engage in a joint task, then some people will override the wishes of others (*e.g.* should we paint the office blue or beige?), and there are bound to be power struggles, faction fights, and all the rest. Even corporations, which have to meet a continuing profit test, have these problems, and the difficulties are bound to increase in non-profit organizations, where there is no instant profit-and-loss feedback. So organizations create problems, so what? So does life itself, or friendships, romantic relationships or whatever. Most people think the drawbacks are worth it, and are more than compensated by the benefits of working for and achieving joint goals. But if not, they can always drop out and not belong to an organization; in a free society, they have that privilege. And of course, we are talking here about voluntary organizations. I suspect Mr. Konkin and his colleagues don't like to join organizations. So be it. But those of us who wish to accomplish various goals will continue to do so. And it seems to me we are at least entitled to the acknowledgment that there is nothing in the slightest unlibertarian about organization, hierarchy, leaders, followers, *etc.* as long as these are done voluntarily. If the Konkinians fail to acknowledge this primordial libertarian point, then their libertarian *bona fides* would come into serious question.

III. THE PROBLEM OF THE "KOCHTOPUS"

Konkin has also railed against the beneficence of Charles Koch, not only for being pro-LP, but *also* because he has tended to acquire a "monopoly" of the movement.

Still abstracting from the LP, let us begin by each one of us putting ourselves in Koch's place. You, say, are a multimillionaire, and you get converted to libertarianism. You're all excited about it, and you want to do something to advance the cause. Things being what they are, the main thing you can contribute is your money. What should you do? The trouble with asking us to make this act of imagination is that most of us can't conceive of ourselves as multi-millionaires, and too many of us have absorbed the primitive populist view of millionaires as evil Fu Manchu characters bent on exploitation. But let's take the case of our multimillionaire convert. Would Konkin *really* say that he should do nothing, because this might create a "monopoly" of the movement? Do we *not* want to convert multi-millionaires, do we *not* think that money is important in advancing the movement? So it is surely grotesque to send our multimillionaire packing. Obviously, we should welcome his contributions to the cause and hope for as much as possible. O.K., so you are a multimillionaire convert to libertarianism. To whom or what should you give your money? Now, this is a considerable responsibility, and since no one can be omniscient our multimillionaire is bound to make mistakes along the way. But all we can ask of him—or ourselves—is to do the best he can, according to his knowledge.

The multimillionaire therefore deserves our approbation, our welcome to the cause. Instead, what he inevitably gets—human nature being what it is—will be complaints and attacks without cease. For if A, B, and C (people or institutions) receive his largesse, this inevitably leaves D, E, and F out in the cold, and whether through envy and/or righteous indignation at the wrong path taken, D, E, and F will no doubt yell bloody murder.

To us poor folk it might seem absurd to say that the life of a multimillionaire is hard and thankless, but it seems clear that this is an important point for us to remember.

But there is more to be said. The critics of the multimillionaire might say: O.K., it's great that he's giving all that money to the cause, but why does he have to *control* everything? But here again, you are the multimillionaire, and you want to do the best you can for liberty with the money you give out. Wouldn't you want to have control over how your own money is spent? Hell yes. You'd have to be an idiot not to, and also not care too much either about money or the libertarian cause. There are few multi-millionaires who are idiots.

But how about the Kochian "monopoly"? Here Mr. Konkin should have fallen back on his Austrian economics. Suppose that only one firm is producing aluminum. Should we start yelling at it for being a "monopoly," or should we hope for *more* firms to enter the industry? Clearly the latter, unless the "monopolist" is using the State to keep other competitors out, which of course Mr. Koch is not doing. Quite the contrary. Koch would be delighted to find other multi-millionaires converted to liberty and giving money to the movement, as would we all. So the answer to the problem of the Koch "monopoly" is to find a dozen more multimillionaire libertarians. It is grossly unfair and fallacious to put the blame on the monopolist for his situation.

I submit that Konkin has been egregiously unfair to Charles Koch. The only legitimate criticism of Koch is not the existence of the "Kochtopus" but if the said "Kochtopus" takes a wrong or misguided track. Within Konkin's anti-party perspective, for example, it is perfectly legitimate for him to criticize Koch's tie-in with the Libertarian Party, but not the existence of Koch largesse *per se*.

In many of Konkin's writings, however, one has the impression that simply the receipt of a grant or the taking of a job with Koch is evil *per se* or, indeed, the taking of any steady job whatsoever (*pace* Konkin on wage-work).

But while there is nothing at all immoral or illegitimate about the existence of a Kochian monopoly in the movement, it does pose grave sociological problems. For if one man or organization constitutes or controls the entire movement, then any mistake of ideology, strategy, or tactics he or it may make will have grave consequences for the entire movement. If a small organization makes a mistake, however, the consequences are not so catastrophic. Here is a real problem, which it is impossible to see how to cure, short of finding a dozen more people like Koch. (Surely, Konkin's putative solution of Koch disappearing from the libertarian scene is a "remedy" far worse than the disease.) The only thing I can think of is trying to persuade Koch to set up "competing" institutions in the movement, much as corporations often set up competing profit centers within their own organization. (To some extent this is already being done, as in the case of such an estimable institution as the Council for a Competitive Economy.)

IV. THE PROBLEM OF THE LIBERTARIAN PARTY

Much of the Konkinian critique of the LP has been conflated with attacks on organization and on "monopoly" *per se*, and I think I have shown that all these criticisms are either fallacious or miss the point—the main point being that these institutions are voluntary and are worth the problems they inevitably bring, at least to those who participate in them. None of these institutions are unlibertarian, and the difficulties they bring in their wake are the problems of life.

We turn to Konkin's *bete noir*, the Libertarian Party. There are two important questions to be resolved about the LP: (1) is it evil *per se*?, and (2) assuming that it isn't, is it a legitimate or even necessary strategy for libertarians to adopt?

I am going to assume for the moment that a libertarian political party (or for that matter, other forms of political action, such as lobbying) are *not* evil *per se*. But if that is true, then all of Konkin's running arguments about the LP's hierarchical nature, its power struggles, faction fighting, *etc.*, are no more than the problems inherent in all organizations whatever. And this we have already disposed of.

More important, I see no other conceivable strategy for the achievement of liberty than political action. Religious or philosophical conversion of each man and woman is simply not going to work; that strategy ignores the problem of power, the fact that millions of people have a vested interest in statism and are not likely to give it up. Violent revolution will not work in a democratic political system. Konkinian agorism is no answer, as I have shown above. Education in liberty is of course vital, but it is not enough; action must also be taken to roll back the state, specifically to *repeal* State laws. Like price control or the withholding tax. Or even like marijuana laws. Despite their widespread non-enforcement, there are always *some* people who get cracked down on, especially if the police wish to frame them for other reasons. Tax rebels are admirable, but only in "micro" terms; the taxes are still there, and the wage-earners pay them. Tax rebellion is not a strategy for victory. Single-issue lobbying groups (*e.g.* anti-draft organizations, taxpayer organizations, gold-standard groups, etc.) are fine and admirable, but they do not complete the job. For two basic reasons: (a) because they are single-issue, and therefore cannot educate anyone in libertarianism across the board; and (b) because they cannot do the vital job of repealing the statist laws. They can only *urge* the repeal of the draft, for example; they can't actually *do* the repealing. Why should we cut ourselves off from this necessary and vital step of doing the repealing? Of course, if one believes with Bob LeFevre that it is *equally* immoral to repeal as to impose the draft, then the repeal of anything is out of the question. But I will shout hosannahs for any repeal of statism, and do not concern myself with the "coercion" of those who'd like to keep the draft and are deprived of it.

Before the existence of the LP, the only repealing could be done by Democrats and Republicans, and so libertarians engaged in this form of political action had to try to find the more libertarian, or rather, the less anti-libertarian candidate. Contrary to Konkin, there *have* been political parties in the past, especially the eighteenth and nineteenth centuries that, while not anarchist, were admirable forces for laissez-faire. They didn't smash the State (not their intention anyway), but they did accomplish an enormous amount for liberty, they ushered in the Industrial Revolution, and we are all in their debt. I think of the Democratic Party in the U. S., the Liberals in England, the Progressives in Germany, *etc.* Historically, classical-liberal political parties have accomplished far more for human liberty than any black markets.

But empirically, of course, neither major party at this point is worth a damn, and so a Libertarian Party provides a welcome alternative, of actually permitting us to engage in libertarian political action.

A Libertarian Party presents many difficulties. For one thing, there is the constant temptation to substitute numbers of votes for profits as the test of success and this means the dilution of principle to appeal to the lowest common denominator of voters. This temptation has been yielded to with great enthusiasm by the Clark campaign. But the price of liberty is eternal vigilance, never more so than in a libertarian political party. The LP needs continual self-criticism and yes, Konkinian criticism as well. Fortunately, it has an admirable platform; now a struggle must get underway to get the party's candidates to stick to that platform. The struggle against opportunism is not going to be easy, and it may not even be successful. But the LP is a valuable enough institution that the battle is worth it. Which is why it needs the Radical Caucus.

And why it needs libertarians who are educated in libertarian principles and are concerned to maintain them. One problem with this particular LP is that in a deep sense it was founded prematurely: before there were enough activists around to make it work and to educate newcomers. The LP grew like Topsy; as a result, very oddly for an ideological party, there are literally no institutions within the Party (except for the Radical Caucus) engaged in education or discussion of principles or political issues. The LP is one of the strangest ideological parties in history; it is an ideological political party where most of its members display no interest whatever in either ideology or politics. Marxist groups generally don't found parties for a long time; first they build "pre-party formations" which gather the strength and the knowledge to launch a regular party. We had no such formation, and are suffering the consequences. But here the party is, and we have to make do with what we have.

So the Libertarian Party is vital if not necessary to repealing statism. And contrary to Konkin's suggested timetable of a millennium, a militant and abolitionist LP in control of Congress could wipe out all the laws overnight. All that would be needed is the will. No other strategy for liberty can work. And yet, all this pales before the most important problem: Is a

Libertarian Party evil *per se*? Is voting evil *per se*? My answer is no. The State is a Moloch that surrounds us, and it would be grotesque and literally impossible to function if we refused it our "sanction" across the board. I don't think I am committing aggression when I walk on a government-owned and government-subsidized street, drive on a government-owned and subsidized highway, or fly on a government-regulated airline. It *would* be participating in aggression if I lobbied for these institutions to continue. I didn't ask for these institutions, dammit, and so don't consider myself responsible if I am forced to use them. In the same way, if the State, for reasons of its own, allows us a periodic choice between two or more masters, I don't believe we are aggressors if we participate in order to vote ourselves more kindly masters or to vote in people who will abolish or repeal the oppression. In fact, I think that we owe it to our own liberty to use such opportunities to advance the cause. Let's put it this way: Suppose we were slaves in the Old South and that for some reason each plantation had a system where the slaves were allowed to choose every four years between two alternative masters. Would it be evil, and sanctioning slavery, to participate in such a choice? Suppose one master was a monster who systematically tortured all the slaves, while the other one was kindly, enforced almost no work rules, freed one slave a year, or whatever. It would seem to me not only *not* aggression to vote for the kindly master, but idiotic it we failed to do so. Of course, there might well be circumstances—say when both masters are similar—where the slaves would he better off not voting in order to make a visible protest—but this is a tactical, not a moral, consideration. Voting would not be evil, but in such a case less effective than the protest.

But if it is morally licit and non-aggressive for slaves to vote for a choice of masters, in the same way it is licit for us to vote for what we believe the lesser of two or more evils, and still more beneficial to vote for avowedly libertarian candidates.

And so there we have it. Konkinian strategy winds up being no strategy at all. Konkin cripples libertarian effectiveness by creating moral problems where none exist: by indicting as non-libertarian or non-market a whole slew of institutions necessary to the triumph of liberty: organization, hierarchy, wage-work, granting of funds by libertarian millionaires, and a libertarian political party. Konkin is what used to be called a "wrecker": let some institution or organization seem to be doing good work for liberty somewhere, and Sam Konkin is sure to be in there with a moral attack.

And yet, Konkin's writings are to be welcomed. Because we need a lot more polycentrism in the movement. Because he shakes up Partyarchs who tend to fall into unthinking complacency. And especially because he cares deeply about liberty and can read-and-write, qualities which seem to be going out of style in the libertarian movement. At least we can count on Sam Konkin not to join the mindless cretins in the Clark TV commercials singing about "A New Beginning, Amer-i-ca." And that's worth a lot.

—Murray N. Rothbard
Nov. 10, 1980

Reply to Rothbard by Samuel Edward Konkin III

Murray N. Rothbard's vigorous assault is refreshing; I'm not sure even I would have taken my first major theoretical attempt seriously if it had not evoked Dr. Rothbard at his trenchant top-of-form. After all, Rothbard and his neo-Romantic view of Ideas almost as clashing super-heroes and villains inspired and maintained many, if not most, of us libertarian activists, most assuredly myself.

Having been offered a field of honour, Rothbard throws the gauntlet down swiftly: "I believe Konkin's agorism to be a total failure." From then on, it's lunge, parry, and slash.

In fine form, Rothbard, alas, is decidedly short of actual weapons. His accusation of a fatal flaw—seemingly *the* fatal flaw—of agorism is so irrelevant to the basis of agorism that it is barely mentioned *en passant* and in a footnote of *New Libertarian Manifesto* (footnote 33, on p. 52, in Chapter III).

Before I dismiss it as criticism of agorism, let me point out that a real debate is justified between Rothbard (and many, many others, to be sure) and me (and quite a few) concerning the validity of hiring out oneself. The *necessity* of it is in question (cybernetics and robotics increasingly replace drudgery—up to and including management activity); the *psychology* of it is in question (selling one's personal activity under another's direction and supervision encourages dependency and authoritarian relationships); and the *profit* in it is open to question (only the rarest skills—acting, art, superscience—command anywhere near the market reward of even low-level entrepreneurship).

Having said that, it remains that this debate is irrelevant in the context of the validity of agorism. Surely, both Rothbard and I would agree on the desirability of increasing the number of entrepreneurs in our society; surely we would both desire more entrepreneurs of libertarianism. Rothbard would simply "let it happen" (*laisser passer*), finding the origins of entrepreneurs mysterious. My own experience is that entrepreneurs are made, not born, and not with that great a difficulty so that "entrepreneurizing (the production of) entrepreneurs" is a profitable activity.

But *ceteris paribus*, as the Maestro says: let us hold the number of entrepreneurs constant. How does that affect agorism? It makes it difficult to convert libertarians to counter-economic entrepreneurialism, but they still can (and ought) to become counter-economic capitalists and workers—even academics! (George H. Smith has blazed trails in becoming a largely counter-economic philosopher!) But when we're talking about converting maybe two million libertarians (at present) to counter-economics and forty million or so counter-economists (already proven to have a strong entrepreneurial component) to libertarianism, the loss of a few thousand extra entrepreneurs seems less than crucial. Moreover, a degree of overlap already exists between libertarians and counter-economists—a *high* degree in my associations.

Again, in passing only, my own observations are that independent contracting *lowers* transactions costs—in fact, it nearly eliminates them relative to boss/worker relationships running the gamut from casual labor with annoying paperwork and records to full-scale Krupp worker-welfarism. But this is an empirical question, one, as Mises would say, not even for economists but economic historians. Why my Austrian credentials should be called into question over such an observation is inexplicable—save as an act of verbal intimidation. *En garde*, then.

And wage-labor's historical benefit may have been as great as the invention of the diaper—but surely toilet-training (in this case, entrepreneurialization) is an even more significant advance?

With the side excursion over, we turn to Counter-Economics, admittedly the basis of agorism and the New Libertarian Strategy. Rothbard finds *NLM* neglecting the "white market"—yet there is one crucial point on which it is most definitely not neglected, either here or in my other Counter-Economic writings. The agorist imperative is to *transform* White into Black. Nothing could be clearer. To do so is to create a libertarian society. *What else can a libertarian society mean* in economic terms but removing market activity from the control of the State? Market activity not under control of the State *is* black market. "Market" activity under the control of the State is white market and we are against it.

To illustrate, slaves building pyramids are white market. Slaves who run away, make deals on the side with stones and tools they have ripped off, and otherwise engage in non-slave activity are black market—and *free* to that extent. What should the libertarian view be toward white-market pyramid building? Or, if you think pyramids would not exist in a free society but aqueducts might, what should our view be toward aqueduct building on the white market *vs* black-market water smuggling? New Libertarians urge the slaves to screw the aqueduct and go for their private buckets until such time as aqueducts can be built under voluntary arrangements. Would Rothbard suggest anything else? Gradual phasing out of aqueduct construction and hence gradual phasing out of slavery?

Rothbard's abolitionist credentials are not challenged, though my own treatment on such matters may impel me otherwise. But a mainly innocent businessman who pays taxes is enslaved to that extent; and is not his going black by dodging or defying the taxes (whichever works best) surely the *immediate* emancipation of this slave? How can Rothbard reject any Counter-Economic moves (that have less than 100% risk of apprehension) by a white marketeer without yielding his abolitionist *bona fides*?

Rothbard's listing of counter-economic services and goods are interesting in one respect: of "jewels, gold, drugs, candy bars, stockings, *etc.*" only one—drugs—is mentioned in the

Manifesto. True, *Counter-Economics* is only now being published chapter by chapter, but even so, the few examples I gave were far more than a few service industries or easily concealed goods. Here is a list, sifted from pages 42 to 45, which *were* mentioned: "food to television repair;" an entire country "Burma is almost a total black market"—this *does* include heavy industry, although Burma has less than the heavy industry of India which is mostly black; the large "black labor" force of Western Europe; housing in the Netherlands; tax evasion in Denmark; currency-control evasion in France; "underground economy" tax-free exchanges in the U.S.; "drugs including laetrile and forbidden medical material"; "prostitution, pornography, bootlegging, false identification papers, gambling, and proscribed sexual conduct between consenting adults;" trucking (the *majority* of this business, by the way); smuggling at all levels; and misdirection of government regulators. None of these are petty. On the contrary, consciously or otherwise on the part of their practitioners, these activities are, in aggregate, big businesses!

Automobiles *are* made counter-economically. Let me count the ways: shipping them across borders (whether physically or on paper) to evade taxes or controls; illegal alien labor for assembly-line production; skimming of parts by management, labor, or even at behest of the owners, which parts then go to produce custom cars; auto plant executives hired as "independent consultants"; design, research, engineering, executive, and computer "consultants" all paid in partial or full counter-economic terms; union "corruption" to make sweetheart deals to avoid labor (State) regulations; OSHA and other inspectors bought off or misdirected; "unsold" product written off inventory and then sold; ... forget it. I cannot possibly count *all* the ways. And next to autos, steel and cement have positively *unsavory* reputations—when it comes to "white collar" crime.

There is a problem of scale here, though. Large, cartelized industries can buy politicians and gain their advantages *directly* from the State. True, anyone about to be apprehended by the State, can, should, and does pay off, bribe, and apply "grease" to the State's enforcers. But what highly competitive industry with a large number of producers can effectively buy votes and politicians—and hence be tempted into using their political clout offensively? *Big* industry in the cartelized sense is no breeding ground for libertarian support but rather for the State's vested interests. However, there is no need to confuse large scale of production with oligopolist characteristics, as Rothbard seems to be doing here.

Finally, as we close out this area, Rothbard accuses me of ignoring the working class. Considering how often he's had the charge leveled at him, one might expect a bit more perceptivity if not sensitivity. What are plumbers, mechanics, carpenters, welders, drivers, farm workers, pilots, actors, accountants, engineers, technicians, lab assistants, computer programmers and plain keypunch operators, nurses, midwives, paramedics and orthomedics (doctors), sales people, public relations people, bartenders, waitresses, writers, factory workers, lawyers, executives, and all types of repairmen if not *workers*, covering the entire spectrum of proletarianism?

All on that list are at least 20% counter-economic and many are over 50%. If they do not take the first step toward economic liberty by becoming independent contractors, then their employer does (tax-free tips for waitresses, off-the-book illegal-alien factory workers, agents handling it for actors, writers, and so on). I challenge Rothbard to find *any legitimate economic field* (not serving the State) that cannot be counter-economized, ten that cannot be counter-economized without organizational or technological innovation, or a hundred that cannot be counter-economized without significant gain in organizational efficiency and profit. "Konkinism" has plenty to say to everyone who is not a statist.

Rothbard's claim that political action is superior and preferable to civil disobedience in lightening the levy is an incredible distortion of history coming from the one who converted *me* to revisionism. There has never been a single repeal of taxation or significant cut (save a few minor ones in recent years for purposes of Keynesian tinkering or Lafferite "less gets more") that did not result from massive refusal to pay or the threat of such disobedience. Furthermore, political action has resulted in shifts in the tax base and higher total plunder—such as the infamously spectacular debacle of Proposition 13 here in California.

Rothbard's agreement with Pyro Egon is ungraciously spurned by Mr. Egon who informs me that what he sees as my "political-like activity" (NLA, MLL) will not generate more entrepreneurs but that entrepreneurs are indeed "makeable." Rothbard, in subsequent correspondence, added that he believes entrepreneurs are born and not made—or at least not makeable.

"Successful entrepreneurs are not going to be agoric theoreticians like Konkin but successful entrepreneurs period. What do they need with Konkin and his group?" How about, "Successful businessmen are not going to be economic theoreticians like Dr. Rothbard but successful businessmen period. What do they need of Dr. Rothbard his group?" Or "Successful engineers are not going to be physics theoreticians like Dr. Einstein..." Or, "Successful writers are not going to be English instructors like Professor Strunk..." Need I belabor the Rothbard fallacy?

Rothbard's position on libertarians being dichotomized from entrepreneurs is absolutely monstrous to me. "Libertarian" has nothing to do with what one *says* but with what one *does*. Hence, libertarians *must* be more trustworthy and have a more rational understanding of the market or they are *not* libertarians regardless of what they beguilingly profess. This is the basis for my muckraking for which Dr. Rothbard commends me. And, on the whole, I find the same lack of black-colored glasses in him, I hasten to add.

And what personal experience or academic study leads Rothbard to conclude that pre-libertarian counter-economists do just fine without agorists "to cheer them on and free them from guilt"? My personal experience leads me to precisely the opposite conclusion—and I have the contributions and letters of gratitude to prove it.

In short, whatever planet the good doctor is describing in contradistinction to my counter-economy surely is not Earth.

Rothbard's statement that violent revolution (what other kind is there against a ruling class—would he like to mention an Establishment that has stepped down peacefully?) has never succeeded in history distorts either the language or history. Either he is saying that no revolution has been libertarian enough to triumph without its contradictions bringing it down (true, but then irrelevant to bring it up as precedent) or he is saying that no group overthrew a ruling class that used democratic means of oppression. The latter is not only false but a direct reversal of history. Nearly all somewhat successful revolutions in recent history have overthrown precisely democratic trappings: American Revolutionaries *vs* the democratic British Imperialists; Jacobin Revolutionaries *vs* the bourgeois *assemble*; Liberal Revolutionaries against the Czar's Duma (March 1917) *and* the Bolshevik revolution against the Liberals and Social Democrats (November 1917); the *falange* against the Spanish Republic (1936); Peron's shirtless ones against the Argentine parliament; the National Liberation Front of Viet Nam *vs* the South Vietnamese parliament (at least until near the end); the popular overthrow of Allende's democratically elected regime (with Pinochet co-opting the revolution for the military); and the recent overthrow of the democratically elected but right-wing president of El Salvador by a centrist "popular" junta.

This list is *not* exhaustive. A claim that "violent revolution" has *only* succeeded in "democratic countries with free elections" would be nearer the mark, and is often used by Latin-American militaries as justification for preventive coups.

All of the above revolutionary groups have their credentials open to libertarian question, to be sure—but who has not so far? To close up this side issue, either Rothbard is saying that all "violent" overthrows of States were not revolutions because they were not libertarian (in which case the libertarian case is untried) or he is historically wrong.

Rothbard has the *chutzpah* to demand that I separate libertarianism from counter-economists because the latter don't need it—and then turn around and ask why the Russian counter-economists have not condensed into agoras. Human action is *willed* action; without entrepreneurs of libertarianism, it will not be sold. Even so, my estimation of the Soviet scene matches that of several Russian dissidents that Russia is a powder keg waiting to go up. The Polish situation, of course, fits the agorist paradigm perfectly, right down to counter-economic workers being co-opted by the partyarch-like Solidarity union.

Rothbard thus fails to make any substantive case against counter-economics and hence against agorist strategy. He shoots at peripherals and warps either language or history to make his case. Still, our disagreement *seems to me* to be largely one of misunderstanding—

and misunderstanding of verifiable facts, not speculative theory. This is hardly surprising since—to my knowledge—we share the same premises and analytic methods. Considering that I adopted mine from his, it is even less surprising.

Rothbard's critique of New Libertarianism seems to rest on seeing tips of icebergs and dismissing the vast bases. He sees only the one percent of the economy thought of as "black market" and not the 20-40% of the economy that the IRS(!) sees as "underground" and double *that* for the rest of the Counter-Economy that the IRS ignores as irrelevant to taxation. It takes a *libertarian*, educated by Rothbard and others, to perceive a common characteristic and sum up the anti-statist whole.

And the same can be said of Rothbard's view of my activities and the hundreds of other New Libertarian Allies around the world. The small but warranted attention we pay to his few deviations seem prominent to him and understandably so. The somewhat larger amount of public criticism we have—of the LP and other activities that interest him most, whether in our publications or at public forums—is what interests him and hence remains foremost in his attention. He has never met the 10,000 people that I conservatively estimate have called themselves libertarians after primary or secondary contact with me and my hard-core allies, and so they are invisible to him. The network of counter-economic businesses that we are painstakingly nurturing and the millions of dollars cumulatively exchanged "invisibly" are likewise understandably invisible to him as well.

I, for one, see no real barrier to re-convergence ("regroupment" as the Marxists would say) between Rothbard (and his "sane, sober, anarchist center") and us "ultra-left deviationists." Rothbard's remaining criticism is really not that germane to the *Manifesto* itself, though it makes up the majority of his article. Yet in some ways it is the most telling criticism of me personally in that it vitiates his compliment to my writing ability when I most obviously failed to communicate effectively. Most of his criticisms of me are misreadings in the latter part, and I will but list and deny them where urgent. Of course, the Party Question is another problem entirely.

New Libertarianism does have an organizational preference. Other forms of organization might then be considered non-New Libertarian but not necessarily "unlibertarian" or even non-agorist. What the New Libertarian Strategy seeks is to optimize action leading to a New Libertarian Society as quickly and cleanly as possible. Activities that lead to authoritarian dependency and passive acceptance of the State are suboptimal and frowned upon; action that is individualistic, entrepreneurial, and market-organized are seen as optimal.

With that constantly in the reader's awareness (pages 54—60 of *NLM* are a long disclaimer to this very point!), it is obvious that there are no moral questions (other than individual self-worth) involved in organization and hierarchy. (My "lumping them all together" that Rothbard decries might be considered integration of concepts by others.)

Nowhere have I ever opposed joint-stock companies (see page 56 again where they are specifically affirmed). *After* I penned *NLM*, I set up precisely that to own *New Libertarian* magazine. I assume we both continue to oppose the statist perversion of joint-stock companies into limited-liability corporations.

I have never suggested "floating affinity groups." Should Dr. Rothbard set up a general Libertarian Alliance that runs no candidates and engages in no Statism, I will take out a hundred-year membership immediately. I urge him to "call me out" on this point.

I see *fewer* problems in organization than does Rothbard and can easily see some organizations not having any.

There is a bit of irony in Rothbard's spirited defense of the "Kochtopus" since his own defection, but I'll let that pass. I have to mention his secession from and opposition to it because that, effectively, ends my major objection to it and I find it relatively harmless and conceivably needing my defense in the near future as the chorus of opposition swells. To the extent that my early attacks are responsible for the demonopolization of the Movement, I am thankful.

For the record, my aim in drawing attention to the monocentrism around Koch's money as spectacularly as I did was a warning. Too many neo-libertarians think that only taking money from the State leads to dependency and control. True, it is not *immoral* in a libertarian sense to become a billionaire's kept writer or lap-activist, but it hardly serves the movement's image *or substance* and hence is un-New Libertarian. I knew the rest of the Left would attack libertarians for being a plutocrat's tool (as *Mother Jones* eventually did) and took action to show the existence of diversity and independence. Offhand, I'd say it worked.

I agree with all of Rothbard's defense of millionaire libertarians and have a few (not *multi*-millionaires, to be sure) in alliance with me. His solution to increase competition in the Movement is and was my solution. I doubt that having Koch compete with himself is a viable answer, though; even Rothbard seems hesitant about suggesting it.

My being "unfair to Charles Koch" requires a bit of semantic care. I have never implied that Charles Koch personally was motivated to do anything. *Anybody* who threw millions into the Movement with a bit of judgment in buying up institutions would have produced the same results.

I'll take Rothbard's and LeFevre's—who know him personally—word that Koch is a great guy. May he profit richly and evade the State forever! (But may he never buy another politician.) And may he contribute to his heart's content to any Libertarian or Libertarian organization (save the LP). Gee, what a great movement when a poor activist such as I can be so generous to an oil billionaire!

But I'll go *further* than Rothbard in my willing recognition of the positive personal characteristics of the Kochtopus. Roy Childs may be cranky and unforgiving at times but he's a fun, erudite person of superior taste, no more deviationist than Dr. Rothbard. Jeff Riggenbach remains a friend, associate, and sometime ally even working full-time for Koch's *Libertarian Review*. Joan Kennedy Taylor, Victoria Varga, Milton Mueller—whom did I leave out?—I've had nothing but enjoyable contacts with them all. Even Ed Crane (Rothbard's—ahem—*bete noir*) is a laugh a minute with a ready handshake and a fast quip, who serves Liberty as he sees best for him and the Movement.

May none of us ever sink to *ad hominem*.

Finally, the Libertarian Party. Rothbard says he will "assume for the moment that a libertarian political party… is *not* evil *per se*." I wonder how open he would be to assuming the State is not evil *per se* and then continuing the discussion of some legislation; let us see where it leads him. It seems to lead to the wonder of repeal of laws.

Rothbard's historical acumen seems to have failed him again. Since when did the State repeal anything from the Corn Laws to suburban property tax *unless it had lost the authority to maintain that law?* First comes countereconomic scofflawing, then mass civil disobedience, then the threat of insurrection, and only *then* repeal. No, I don't agree with LeFevre that it is *immoral* to repeal the draft (assuming LeFevre would say precisely that) but it is immoral to support politicians to oppress us because they *might* relieve *one* oppression. For all the money, time, and energy that needs to go into electing a politician good on one or a few issues, how many people could be directly freed and their risk of apprehension reduced in tax evasion, draft evasion, regulation evasion, and so on? Nor do you need exhort the evaders to contribute to a noble cause but simply offer—and some sell this for exorbitant fees!—instruction on how to do beat detection and watch them go for it… *freeing themselves*, not being freed by someone else.

Votes *are* the "profits" of a political party. A party is an organ of the State whose overt purpose is to vie for control of the State and whose covert one is to co-opt support—to gain the sanction of the victim. The number of votes dictate the number of successfully elected officials *and* their share of power and plunder; *and* the number of those still accepting the State's legitimacy and possible usefulness. Crane and the Clark Campaign were only acting in accordance with their nature *qua* partyarch. As Frank Chodorov might have said, "The way to get rid of sellouts in LP jobs is to get rid of LP jobs."

Let's take up those political parties Rothbard *now* finds admirable. It is clear that the Democrats were not so lovable in *Conceived in Liberty* when, as Jefferson Republicans, they fought the Anti-Federalists and co-opted opposition to the Constitution. Did Jackson, the agent of Nullification's defeat; Van Buren, the archetype of boss politics; Polk, the anti-Mexican imperialist; or Pierce and Buchanan, the defenders of slavery, redeem this tainted beginning?

And the British Liberals were condemned by Rothbard for leading Liberty's advocates into defense of Empire and World War. Nor did the moderate minarchists of the time—let alone the many anarchists even then—have any use for Democrats or Liberals. Those minarchist reformers were then in the Free Soil Party in the U.S. and the Philosophic Radical Party in Britain, respectively.

It would be *gauche* of me to remind Dr. Rothbard just who invented the Radical Caucus and then discarded it when it served nothing but "objectively counter-revolutionary" ends, so I'll pass this section up.

"A militant and abolitionist LP in control of Congress" begs the question—how did it get there? How *could* it get there? George Smith's scenario seems far more plausible. In fact, the LP *will* be in power during the final stages of agorist revolution to lure away our marginal allies and ensnare the unwary with "Libertarian" newspeak. The LP will be put in power as soon as the Higher Circles need it there. I have no doubt that Dr. Rothbard will be the first to notice and denounce the collaboration.

Can you imagine slaves on a plantation sitting around voting for masters and spending their energy on campaigning and candidates when they could be heading for the "underground railway"? Surely they would choose the counter-economic alternative; surely Dr. Rothbard would urge them to do so and not be seduced into remaining on the plantation until the Abolitionist Slavemasters' Party is elected.

Rothbard's characterizing me as a "wrecker" is truly surprising to me considering all the libertarian organizations and publications I have built up and supported—more than anyone else save Dr. Rothbard himself; from Wisconsin to New York to California, and in nearly every state, province, and country on this globe. Am I supposed to list all the libertarian groups that have *not* been subjected to moral attacks by me? How about every libertarian supper club in Los Angeles and New York? The Society for Individual Liberty, Society for Libertarian Life, the old California Libertarian Alliance and Texas Libertarian Alliance, the British Libertarian

Alliance, the Future of Freedom Conference, the Southern Libertarian Conference... oh, this is ridiculous. Yes, I have stopped beating my wife—even if I'm not married.

The only things I have wrecked are the wreckers of our once party-free movement, the defence of partyarchy, and the compromise of libertarianism in general. Is Rothbard claiming that he averted his eyes from those leaving "The Plumb Line" because they might otherwise do good work?

In conclusion, Rothbard and I continue to fight for the same goals—and against the same enemies. I hope we will continue to fight in our own ways, reaching those whom others may have missed. And the greatest hope is that we may reduce our time and energy spent on fighting each other, in order that we may free up resources to turn against the common enemy. I shall pass up no hand outstretched.

If the New Libertarians and the Rothbardian Centrists must devote some time to our differences ("engage in Revolutionary Dialogue"), let it be devoted first to *understanding* each other—as this exchange is intended—and then to resolving those differences. Ah, then let the State and its power elite quake!

—Samuel Edward Konkin III

Return to Babylon by Robert LeFevre

Samuel Edward Konkin's *New Libertarian Manifesto* falls short of literary acclaim and fails, at least in my judgment, of sounding a clarion call for the Libertarian cause. This does not imply lack of value or meaning.

The thirty-one pages of small print has definite merit in a number of places and here and there flashes of wisdom illumine a passage.

The author is to be commended for his clear grasp of economic principles and his devotion to marketplace procedures to the extent that he pursues them. This is the major achievement emerging from the so-called "old left" and hopefully signals a burgeoning return to sanity for those who, in earlier days, suffered from internal bleeding, but whose "cure" was the senseless leveling of everyone and everything in society which had managed despite the odds to continue to stay afloat.

Konkin's dedication to what he calls Agoric tactics conveys the substance of his position. It means, in short, that individual libertarians are capable of acting now within a free market context, if they don't permit fear of government to inhibit them altogether. This position deserves to be applauded until the sound echoes and I heartily lend my support to it.

A word of caution should be inserted. The Konkin Manifesto is not the proper place for such advisory words and my addition does constitute a criticism of that document. But it is high time something were said, and this appears to be an appropriate place to say it.

If Agoric enterprises are to make the impact they deserve to make, libertarian enterprisers are going to have to do a *better* job than their competitors already in the field. Thus far, they are not doing it.

Price advantage and a chance to avoid the state by tax evasion is no substitute for integrity. Many who appear as Agoric enterprisers have cheated or otherwise betrayed their customers. Indeed, I have personally found it necessary to be especially careful when dealing with a person calling himself libertarian. All too often, the self-styled libertarian has demonstrated a lack of concern for even fundamental honesty. Many have already experienced this lack among conventional marketeers and more of the same is not helpful.

While I would not personally subscribe to the practice, many would-be customers of Agoric enterprises discover to their dismay that if they are cheated through black market patronage, legal action against their suppliers is out of the question. Agoric enterprises cannot succeed without building customer confidence. Persons who are cozened into buying simply because of a warm fellow-feeling philosophically, lose both the feeling and the philosophy when confronted with misrepresentation, poor quality and deception with no recourse.

Indeed, the merit of any philosophy is discovered by the character of its adherents. In this regard, it is clear that many who say they are libertarians are merely employed in obtaining protective coloration.

The foregoing, while not a criticism of the *Manifesto*, opens the door. The ordinary mortal, considering the condition we are in; dominated and coerced by the state at every hand, has tended insensibly to equate all government legislation with repression. But the government is an octopus of many tentacles. There are any number of laws on the books of the state condemning dishonesty, misrepresentation, and violence. These are actions which should be repressed; but, of course, repressed by the discipline and determination of the individual.

When disobedience to government is recommended *per se* and *ad hoc*, it is a simple matter for the individual to conclude that dishonesty, misrepresentation and violence are acceptable forms of conduct since the state is "always" wrong. There are thousands who fail to make the distinction that while the state is wrong in its methods and procedures in every case, the ends ostensibly sought may very well be desirable and necessary.

The *Manifesto* is lacking at this point. Breaking the law is not a virtuous act *per se*, but the *Manifesto* makes it appear so. Thus, it may well occur that some simplistic minds, thinking to obstruct the state, will conclude that any action they take which violates some government ukase is commendable.

The state has been far more clever than many suppose. It has mixed virtue and non-virtue in its demands. But it has used all its instruments of propaganda to cause both the dull and the simplistic to believe that everything that is morally proper is demanded by the state. Thus, law and morals have been inextricably intertwined. To break the law has become immoral; to obey it, moral. Neither is necessarily the case. The objective of a given enactment must be examined for its intrinsic character. With the state we must deal constantly with both ends and means. The means of the state are corrosive and vicious without exception. Libertarians are among those who supposedly have the necessary acumen to determine the difference between ends and means.

Thus, they should be able to practice self-discipline by overt demonstration that they are more honest than those who are only honest because the state appears to compel it.

Indeed, this confusion arising from inappropriate means employed to achieve desirable ends may well be the most profound reason why the state cannot attain its objectives. It is at this point that the *Manifesto* achieves its greatest height. Konkin's explanation of the mandatory use of desirable means that will achieve desirable ends is superb. He champions consistency. It is the core of his opposition to such alleged "libertarian" activities as political party activism.

One of the major objections that I must voice relates to the position taken in the *Manifesto* concerning restoration and/or restitution, following the commission of a crime. While I will quickly assert that Konkin's explanation is both lucid and brief, it does not square with his insistence upon a harmony between ends and means.

If each individual human being has a right to his own life and property then it follows that no individual has a rightful claim to the life or property of any other. In his zeal to satisfy the wishes of those who say they have been victimized, Konkin sets forth an argument, sometimes brilliant, sometimes sophist, in which it appears that the individual, having rights to his own life and property, loses those rights if and when he violates the property boundary of another.

If such a conclusion is valid, then it follows that the only persons who have rights are persons who do not violate property boundaries. If this proposition is accepted, then the concept of rights applies only to a limited number of persons and it is based upon their behavior and not upon their nature as human beings.

Now the fundamental nucleus around which the notion of rights orbits is that the concept must universally apply or be meaningless. If the concept of rights is to be delimited, applying only to those persons who behave in a specific manner, then we have a concept of privilege and not a concept of rights.

If we are to accept the notion of privilege as the core to our social structure, we are at once reverted to feudalism. Only those who behave as the Lord dictates have the privilege of living. The Lord has the "divine" right to eliminate others, since they had no rights of their own in the first place.

But Konkin wastes little time on such niceties. Rather, he makes it appear that the criminal has not only lost his rights, but that his victim has gained rights over him and, thus, the victim, to a large degree, becomes the owner and possessor of the criminal and may dispose of him according to the wishes of the victim, ameliorated perhaps by the pleas of a third-party insurer or other arbitrator.

This is the argument of the Statist. But having denounced the State in the most specific and conclusive terms, Konkin now embraces the state procedures as a major virtue. While it is wrong for the state to claim the life or property of anyone because no one is the property of the state, it is entirely acceptable for the victim to lay claim to restitution and restoration at the cost of the criminal. Indeed, Konkin describes restitution and restoration as a *moral imperative*. But that is what the state says.

Then, citing Rothbard and the Tannehills as pioneers in this area, Konkin offers us a paragraph which I repeat here in its entirety so that its character can be judged.

> First, always leaving out those who choose not to participate, one insures oneself against aggression or theft. One can even assign a value to one's life in case of murder (or inadvertent manslaughter) which may range from the taking of the violence-initiator's life to taking replaceable organs (technology willing) to restore life, to the payment to a foundation to continue one's life work. What is crucial here is that the victim assigns the value of his life body, and property *before* the mishap. (Exchangeable goods may simply be replaced at market rate. See below.)

If I understand this proposal, the victim of a crime gains a property right, not only over the criminal's property, but, depending on the nature of the crime, over the criminal's person and even the criminal's life.

Further, and based upon what has gone before as well as upon the quotation used, it is morally mandatory that the victim get back *more* than was taken from him. It is this margin that is viewed as a deterrent against future crime.

Somehow, at this juncture, I wish that Konkin was less familiar with science fiction. I am swept back to my boyhood days and the wonderful stories of Edgar Rice Burroughs, most particularly his classic Mastermind of Mars—Ras Thavas—and his protagonist, Vad Varo.

The *Manifesto* has invited us to travel in time in an effort to recognize the magnificence of a truly libertarian society. I have found it astonishingly easy to comply. By the arguments given I am not only reverting to my teens and *The Warlord of Mars*, I am swept back to Babylon and an oriental despot named Hammurabi. What the *Manifesto* is calling a libertarian society was existent at that time, some 3800 years ago. There were no police. They were invented in the 19th century by Sir Robert Peel in Britain.

Hammurabi, as it turned out, had a kind of restitution/restoration agency. Historians have generally agreed that it could be termed the principle of "an eye for an eye; a tooth for a tooth."

While the *Manifesto* invites us to travel both backward and forward in time, the result that I see takes us backward to Babylon and there we are beached. We will not only have "an eye for any eye; a tooth for a tooth," we will have liver for liver, spleen for spleen, a kidney, heart, or gall bladder for its counterpart.

Unless I am grossly incapable of understanding the words employed, I see here a chamber of horrors so brutal and heinous that by comparison Torquemada's rack and thumbscrew become a taffy pull and manicure.

But let me set the sadism aside for a moment and consider the consequences of such a system. Given this concept as a *modus vivendi*, millions of people will wish to become victims! Crimes can be staged which haven't occurred. Incriminating evidence can be planted. Indeed, I can envision schools conducted by various Fagins engaged in encouraging the perpetration of pseudo-aggression.

The possibilities are endless. What a marvelous way of bringing an enemy to ruin. Accuse him of having imposed an injury upon you. Take care that you purchase a few witnesses and plant a bit of evidence, and you have a profitable business. Indeed, like the criminal class in Egypt, you can permit yourself to be maimed and made grotesque. It insures generous alms and a good living.

We are now back to Shakespeare and *The Merchant of Venice*. After all, the request of Shylock was the fulfillment of his bond. And this would be warranted in what the *Manifesto* calls a "libertarian" system. In this strange system, Antonio will die under the knife, and the blood shed, although not mentioned in the bond, will constitute "profit" to the victim; that marginal deterrent.

To offset this, the *Manifesto* and its supporters will have to write a series of elaborate laws to identity, define, and specify a pretended crime as a crime in itself. Excluding semantics, what makes such a procedure different from that of every state in existence?

If such a procedure is not followed, then we will have each insurance company engaged in filling each contract with fine print as to what is and what is not a crime, as set forth by the directors of that company. I see small merit in competition toward brutality.

Indeed, this has been the bane of nearly every effort made by alleged Anarchists of whom I have knowledge. They decry the state. They vilify the state. They excoriate it. It will be abolished. And in place of it they tell us we will have a system in which precisely the same remedies are sought by processes which include the use of violence and the violation of men's minds, bodies, and property. But we won't call it a state! It will be an Insurance Company. Or a Protection Company. Or a Restoration, Restitution, Retaliation Ragout.

Alas, there is still more.

I am told (page 30, paragraph 1), "Only at this point, when the matter has been fully *contested, investigated*, and *judged*, and *still* B (the aggressor) refuses to relinquish the stolen property, would violence occur."

If we take a look at the real world, we will discover that if B (the aggressor) doesn't wish to be a contestant and refuses to be investigated, coercion must be employed long before judgment is rendered. If B will not permit entry into his home, where the victim alleges he has seen his stolen property, then, to verify the allegation, force must be used to win B's compliance. But what if, in fact, B is guilty of nothing except that he looks like the aggressor, or that what was allegedly stolen had a duplicate which B has honestly acquired? Then we find an innocent person, seeking to maintain his privacy and go about his business peacefully, victimized by an investigative company merely to please the wishes of A, who, in fact, may not even have experienced an act of theft but wishes to destroy the credibility of B.

The true nature of B cannot be determined prior to an investigation. And a contest, and a judgment. But these things cannot be obtained without coercion, if B is unwilling. The guilty conceivably would always be unwilling. But many who are innocent would likewise be unwilling. Or will willingness be law?

The suggestion is made that we can have prison camps for the recalcitrant (but not prisons) and that here and there we can always kill the person who has (it is alleged) himself performed some act of killing.

Isn't this a clear case of asking the ends to justify the means? It appears so, at which point we have waved goodbye to consistency.

I find it difficult to come up with a dollar scale by means of which to set a price on life, consent to intimacy, and non-kidnapping.

Indeed, and for reasons Konkin has set forth, I find it difficult, if not impossible, to come up with a dollar value even for stolen property. A single dollar has a different value to different people, depending on their relative scales of value, for dollars, goods, and services.

Thus, as Konkin correctly shows, value judgments enter in and restitution and restoration must be *arbitrarily* imposed as a deterrent. Indeed, this appeals to be the primary rationale for asking for *more* than a mere restoration or restitution. Since it would be impossible to arrive at a condition identical to that which preceded the crime, then error will be made but it must be made on behalf of the victim.

This insistence of establishing property rights over the perpetrator of a crime appears to overlook the fact that, on occasion, a crime may be committed because of dire financial conditions. Such conditions will *always* manifest in any world of limited resources and imperfect human beings. While the "old left" attempted to make it appear that *all* crime arose from poverty (absurd on its face) the fact remains that some crimes have always been caused by privation. If a person is starving he will very possibly steal, even if he has to inflict physical injury on an innocent bystander in process.

I do not condone theft because of this fact. Any act of theft is a wrongful act, regardless of motivation. But I see nothing within the *Manifesto* which takes such a possibility into consideration. The criminal is a criminal; the victim is a victim. A rose, is a rose, is a rose.

Konkin has been both generous and gracious in the *Manifesto* concerning my own position for which I thank him. Further, he is at least partly correct in stating (footnote 15, page 23) "LeFevre's pacifism also dilutes the attraction of his libertarian tactics, probably far more than deserved."

That my position tends to turn away many is confirmed. That I deserve better is a moot point.

But I have never taken a position with the view to making it popular. Every statement I have made I have tried to make consistent with truth and with the fundamental definition of human liberty. I have not called for a following. I have found my own way and would not deprive a single person of the joy he can experience by finding his.

Konkin is correct when he observes in the same footnote that: "He (LeFevre) holds back from describing a complete strategy resulting from these personal tactics, partially due to a fear of being charged with *prescribing* as well as *describing*."

The strategy which I have repeatedly set forth does not and will not appear to be a strategy for those who insist on group action. They can conceive of no strategy deserving of the name until people are somehow welded into a group.

The strategy I have offered goes hand in hand with the tactics I also recommend. It is the same one-on-one procedure which assists each individual in removing himself without violence from the cloying, clutching tentacles of all states. While admittedly it cannot be done either instantly or perfectly, it can be achieved by those who wish to achieve it. I make no apology for its imperfections. Agoric enterprises aren't perfect either, and never will be. Humanity does not produce perfect specimens.

Finally, I come to what I view as a second inconsistency in the *Manifesto*. Encouraged by the author's invitation, let me point to it.

In passing through the various phases which Konkin's imagination has portrayed, we come at last to the transition between phase 3 and 4.

Konkin sees this period as inevitably violent, in total betrayal of the very principles he claims to espouse.

"Revolution is as inevitable as any human action can be," is Konkin's footnote assertion. So, in the end, regardless of peaceful means, we must throw out the Agoric principles of self-fulfillment and kill the statists as the only way to a free society.

Konkin acknowledges that there are arguments against this view. Personally, I believe it is Konkin's philosophic origin in left-of-center areas which causes him to cling to this position.

The primary reasons I should like to offer, which in my view significantly alter the "inevitability" he sees, relate to the method he uses of advancing Agoric causes, and the nature of capitalism in all forms including the Agoric.

By employing the one-on-one educational method, the gradual resurgence of free enterprise will advance only as rapidly as our ability to educate makes it possible. Thus, free market principles are never imposed, they are learned and proven by those who learn and practice.

An uninhibited marketplace is far more profitable and comfortable than an inhibited marketplace. The assertion that "Statists" will adhere to statism neglects the reality of a major characteristic of all Statists.

They, too, seek profit. They seek applause, recognition, and comfort. As the Agoric principles unfold and enlarge by the adding of dedicated practitioners, moving in that direction becomes expedient. All statists are given to expedience and seek the high ground. There will be a natural tendency for the most ambitious and most capable statists to move in that direction.

To be successful in any kind of free market, Agoric or conventional, capital investments must be made. No one with capital invested can afford the risks to capital destruction and divestiture entailed in war. And in this context take note: All wars are state-inspired. But they are invariably directed against *another state*, not against the politicians of the local state. Politicians don't *wage* war. They *make* the war by encouraging conflict which keeps them out of harm's way. Part of the politician's "capital" is the sanction he has obtained from his own countrymen, and part consists of his pose of super-intelligence which must be protected by the sacrifice of others. He will risk more by violent conflict than by moving in the direction of free enterprise.

I am delighted to see the Konkin Manifesto and can applaud it *in general* for its position respecting consistency, objective, and method. My objections, if understood, may heighten its impact. I believe it will have and deserves to have a compelling influence upon members of the "old" left. Here its syntax and its sometimes purple passages may well be pivotal in any number of instances. I wish it and its author well.

—Robert LeFevre
October 1980

REPLY TO LEFEVRE
BY
SAMUEL EDWARD KONKIN III

In one sense, there is little to say to Robert LeFevre's reply to *New Libertarian Manifesto*. His position and potential response was put forward in *NLM*, as he himself observes accurately, and he responded pretty much as predicted. Our area of agreement and disagreement remains the same.

LeFevrians are welcome in a New Libertarian society; the converse may not be true but since they have, for consistency, prevented themselves from doing anything about us, we can live together. Of course, the LeFevrians need fear nothing from New Libertarians; what will excite their righteous indignation, ire, and possible shunning is that we will defend ourselves against aggressors. Since the pure LeFevrians will never be aggressors, they will wax wroth over the injuries or possible injuries to murderers, thieves, burglars and rapists—with the heroic self-defenders being the object of their wrath. Their stingless buzzing, I hasten to add; their biteless bark.

LeFevre has done more to increase our ranks than any individual other than Murray Rothbard. It is truly instructive in the diversity of the Movement of Libertarians to see the total *orthogonality* of his critique of *NLM* compared to Rothbard's. The two views are perpendicular with no overlap. LeFevre accepts what Rothbard rejects and *vice versa*, although there is an area in the later, advanced section that both are, expectedly, unsure of.

Although LeFevre has radicalized and galvanized hundreds of thousands of libertarians, a clear majority of them remain detached from his pacifism, even though it is his core, and absorb the outer layers of his ideology—which turn out to be very pure libertarianism. His presentation is superb, due to his will, skill, and actor's training.

One characteristic about LeFevre's position often neglected is all the innovations he has introduced to the philosophy. The pacifist principle drives him to find the most ingenious methods to accomplish protection, defense, and evasion of aggression. A few of the best of his followers or students who remain true to his basic position—Richard Radford, Caroline Roper-Deyo, Linda Abrams, Sy & Riqui Leon, and Harry Browne come readily to mind—show the same ingenuity and innovative tendency. We self-defending libertarians can put up with an awful lot of annoyance at being hectored about our violent tendencies or rhetoric in exchange for the value of the product of that pacifist-motivated research. The less to be spent on the overhead of self-defense, the better; could anything be closer to a "universal good"?

Given all that, LeFevre deserves to be answered. In fact, not to answer directly his attacks—as many libertarian theorists choose—is a form of condescension he certainly does not deserve. Frankly, I think his position is wrong and obstinately so, given all the evidence he has had to face. But there is nothing ignoble or demeaning about it.

Putting the pacifism principle in one's mind seems to have the effect of ingesting a psychoactive drug. Flashes of brilliant insight and otherwise-inconceivable innovation and invention result, but mostly what comes out is a distorted view of reality. This view seems warped to the "straight" observer though it makes perfect sense to the psychonaut. Yet, with time and observations, the internal logic to the warp is discernible to the observer.

Passing over the mutual appreciation section of LeFevre 's reply—and we do concur in much—one comes to the criticism. Of course it is assumed that one has read *New Libertarian Manifesto* before reading this, but even so, a translation of LeFevre 's "warp factor" may help no end.

First, as far as lecturing libertarians on integrity and making sure they know I'm not telling them to break natural law, I do not believe a *libertarian* could possibly read *NLM* and think otherwise. Perhaps some non-libertarian might see such a call to indiscriminate "lawbreaking," but I'm clearly not the one to reach those with such a lack of reasoning ability. Perhaps we need anarcho-therapists for those whose brains have been turned to jelly by overdoses of statism? And while I may have been burned as often as LeFevre in market transactions with alleged libertarians, I have prepared for sale appropriate "White Lists" of untrustworthy types. As whitelisting is developed by the counter-economy, the ripoff rate should rapidly fall. I consider the burns I have experienced to be the start-up costs of the agora.

LeFevre's point about legal action being out of the question after a black-market burn has a strange ring. Surely *legal action is out of the question for LeFevrians* in any market, white, grey, or black. In fact, even though not LeFevrians in general, New Libertarians urge defensive and restorative remedies entirely outside the State's legal system *in all circumstances.* No one could possibly threaten you with as much aggression as the State; calling on the State to eliminate a mugger is like summoning Satan to exorcise an imp.

Our parting of the ways begins where LeFevre sees "good laws" on the books of the State—and that ties in with his later claim that agorists would need a legal system to enforce restoration of property. What he seems to fail to perceive in New Libertarians and most other anarchist libertarians is that we object to the *nationalization* of the "business of justice" by the State. There are *no* laws that the State could have in common with a market agency because the former must *legislate* with *statist execution* written into the law. Market restorers and protectors will follow Natural Law—which is discovered by observation, like any phenomenon in nature—and apply the *natural* response, or the optimal one among many.

Moving onward, we find a pæan to self-discipline: hear, hear.

When LeFevre challenges me on consistency, however, he does strike to the quick. He claims that I accept the right to one's life and property and then deny it to an aggressor. But if I yielded up the property of the victim to the aggressor—when I could restore it—*then* I would be violating my consistency. As far as I am concerned, the aggressor has opened the boundary of his property (not just "land" property we're talking about) and opened up a passage to the stolen property *which is and was never within his boundary,* which I reseal after regaining the missing item(s).

The aggressor has *voluntarily* chosen to open that path. The victim has agreed to nothing. Should the victim neglect any retrieval of her or his goods, I have the right delegated to do so. The sanction of the aggressor is given to the victim the moment the attack is initiated by the will of the aggressor.

LeFevre chooses to look at the world from the irrational eyes of the aggressor who wishes to initiate his action and be free of its consequences. I have no intention of faking reality for the violence-initiator. Perhaps he can evade apprehension for his theft or attack as one who jumps a cliff can be wafted away on a strong updraft; but the natural consequence of gravity is to fall to one's death and the natural consequence of invasion is restoration.

To make it perfectly clear where LeFevre and I differ, I see no rights of the aggressor being violated by restorative action. If one beats one's fist against a rock and bleeds, are one's rights violated? The same natural law applies to striking those who can and do defend themselves successfully.

No privilege is established. No feudalism—whose prime characteristic was preventing the serf from defending himself against the lord's plunder through quasi-religious mystification of power relations—exists. Nor has the "criminal" lost his *rights* nor do I make it appear thus—the "criminal" merely has failed to gain any "rights"—unearned privileges—over the victim.

Nor is this the "argument of the Statist." The argument of the Statist has ever been to disarm those who would defend themselves. Substituting themselves (the statists) as defenders is only one ploy they use and a secondary one at that. There have been many anarchists who have denounced pacifists as counter-revolutionary precisely because they objectively serve the State at that point. Since New Libertarians consider non-aggression primary and fighting the State secondary, we accept pacifists as sometime allies. But should it ever happen that a LeFevrian actually convinces anarchists not to eliminate the State when they could, he will receive anything but my gratitude and can live with all the slaughter and plunder that continues.

The State does *not* say that restitution and restoration are *moral imperatives*. The State—everywhere, in all forms—rejects restoration in favor of punishment, "rehabilitation" (*i.e.* thought control), and execution. Anything *but* restoration is acceptable to the State.

And as we move along, we find horror on LeFevre's part over the aggressor's possibly losing an organ if technology could use it to restore a victim. My heart goes out to the crippled and dying victims, not to the obscenity of a hale and hearty thug standing over his prey, withholding the ability to restore the sufferer. I would swallow my normal aversion to biological lab practices and gleefully wield the scalpel's first stroke! LeFevre can live with himself and the dying victim's gasps if he would not do likewise.

Hammurabi did *not* have anything approaching a restitution/restoration agency; he had its frustrator and enemy, the State.

So far, then, we deal with different worldviews based on defence *vs* pacifism. The debate is stimulating and fair. But then LeFevre *seems* to dump the Marquis of Queensbury. What he sneaks in is the problem of error, of misinterpretation of evidence and being deliberately misled. My response is *tu quoque!* Suppose LeFevre is blowing up stumps on his farm and was led to believe that no one was near—perhaps quite reasonably. Perhaps someone parachuted down in the seemingly safe field and *boom!* LeFevre discovers the mangled remains.

And what if someone wants to get rid of an enemy and leads them to the next stump to go, then rushes to assure LeFevre that all is clear?

Why should I feel any greater problem with errors in restoration than he sees in any other problems in living? And why should he then bring it up? Surely we will always do our best to act safely. The world is constructed such that human action will always contain the *risk* of accidental violence done to another. In the agorist world, prompt restoration would be the best indicator of an accident's nature.

No series of elaborate laws need be written. Natural Law seems blazingly obvious and simple to me and to most disputants for the past thousands of years—lawyers, LeFevre, and David Friedman notwithstanding.

Asking the ends to justify the means is, by every definition I know, what consistency means. The only other possibility is to have ends and means be *inconsistent*. Nor *must* restoration and restitution be *arbitrarily* imposed; I *oppose* precisely that in Chapter Two at some length, showing how the market can be used to establish a value. I also explicitly oppose any imposition of fines or anything else for deterrent value over what deterrent is naturally contained in full restitution costs (including interest and apprehension). Hardly cricket of LeFevre to suggest I did otherwise.

And to close off this area finally, New Libertarians have no "insistence of establishing property rights over the perpetrator of the crime" as LeFevre would have it. In fact, again, *New Libertarian Manifesto* insists on *the opposite*—no property rights over any individual ever. Only that in which the victim already has rights is to be restored. But no less than her or his rightful property—all of it. Let LeFevre answer a moral charge for a change: what gives him the right to yield up another's property *right*, especially to the one who deserves it least?

It is fairly clear from my previous statements and articles and accolades for LeFevre that I have no quarrel with *his* strategy. In fact, as a *tactic* I endorse and practice it fully with the highest success of any tactic. I urge other New Libertarians to sell others "one-on-one" if they have any talent for salesmanship. But without a *strategy* in the package they're offering to sell in this tactical maneuver, there are a lot fewer customers. Here, Rothbard is right.

LeFevre's hold on reality—or at least the world I thought we shared—gets pretty tenuous near the end. Crimes are never *caused* by privation. They are *caused* by the will—and willfulness—of an acting individual. Period. Including the crime of statism. Why should my observation that the transition from Phase 3 to Phase 4 involves violent revolution "betray" any of *my* principles when I make it blindingly clear that it is the *State* that will initiate the violence without fail? If I am to take no action to defend myself, I may be a brave pacifist; but if I flee from the right path because I am threatened with violence then I am simply a coward. Surely LeFevre would not have me shrink from the agorist society's fulfillment because *others* threaten violence? I am not responsible for what they in their compulsive evil do—regardless of how predictable I find it.

Finally, I have no origin in left-of-center areas, having followed a path to libertarianism from right-wing statism similar to LeFevre's. Perhaps he refers to my greater familiarity with State-Leftist argument due to broader reading? I urge him to widen his background similarly.

I see no threat of forceful imposition of free-market principles; the act is self-contradictory.

And I am glad that LeFevre can read the minds of hard-core statists better than I, because we can certainly use his telepathic powers to gather intelligence from the enemy camp. Nonetheless, LeFevre's idea about the State making war only against other States is quickly tossed in history's ample dustbin: what of the conquests by imperialist states of anarchies in Ireland, Iceland, and Iboland? What of the countless crushings of internal insurrections in every state's history *including this one* from the Whiskey Rebellion of the 1790s to the Civil War of the 1860s to the Days of Rage of the 1960s?

All said and done, this brief reply really is exhaustive of LeFevre's ideological flaws. Fortified with the knowledge of what to filter from his generally superb body of original libertarian work, the student of libertarianism should feel free to dive deeply into the heady waters of uncut, pure LeFevrian thought.

Perhaps the greatest compliment I can return to him is to conclude that after *New Libertarian Manifesto* weathers a frontal assault by LeFevre—and a full flank one by Rothbard—it will withstand any lesser sortie.

—Samuel Edward Konkin III

The New Altruism: A Critique of *New Libertarian Manifesto* by Erwin S. "Filthy Pierre" Strauss

I have little quarrel with the basic vision of society presented in *New Libertarian Manifesto*: "an advanced counter-economic system (approaching) the free society" (note on page 24). I also agree that the "free society" itself would be unstable for the reasons you give in paragraph 3 on page 25. However, as pro-agoric activity broadens from individual actions, business enterprises, *etc.*, toward the explicit pursuit of grand strategy through a continental "Movement," a problem arises. At some point, the link between what an individual puts into the activity (in terms of scarce resources, such as labor or money) and what the individual can expect to get out (in terms of increased freedom) begins to break down. The broader "Movement" activities deal in increasingly public goods. The benefits of "an advanced counter-economic system as it nears the free society" will be enjoyed just as much by those who did not contribute scarce resources toward its achievement as by those who did. Therefore, it is difficult rationally to justify making such a contribution, which would involve incurring a significant cost in exchange for (at best) a microscopic increase in the expected value to oneself of a good (increased freedom) to be received in the future.

It seems to me that the people likely to contribute to such a "Movement" will be those motivated by altruism. That is, they will be those who are interested in living their lives for the sake of others. In other words, they will be those people who are prepared to set the costs incurred by themselves off against the benefits conferred on other people, as if those benefits had been conferred on themselves. This is a good economic definition of altruism.

Now, I myself am not categorically opposed to altruism. I recognize that the genes and/or deep cultural values embodied in me evolved in certain contexts. These contexts selected for genes and/or values that gratified their bearer for seeking certain goals. These goals include such things as eating sweet foods, copulating with members of the opposite sex—and advancing the interests of other bearers of the same genes and/or values (i.e., altruism). I recognize that these goals may, in general, be at cross-purposes with my rational self-interest in the present context. Nevertheless, up to a point, the most efficacious policy for me may be to appease those values, if this can be done at reasonable cost. However, as the scarce resources devoted to such appeasement increase, there comes a point where further appeasement of those values constitutes paying an excessive price for ephemeral psychological values. At that point, it is time to stop such indulgences and get down to work pursuing more substantial goals.

However, I *am* categorically opposed to logical contradiction. You set yourself up as categorically opposed to altruism (e.g., in "Our Enemy, The Party," you call it immorality—though it would be personal immorality, rather than the social immorality you group it with, as long as it involves no coercion). But in the *Manifesto*, you say you count yourself among those "who burn for Liberty, and wish to devote themselves to that life's work" (page 55). But Liberty does not exist in the abstract; it is enjoyed by specific people. The set of those people for whose Liberty you burn either contains nobody besides yourself, or it contains other people. If the former, then your earlier statement on page 54 applies: "For those who wish only to live their lives as free as possible ... counter-economic libertarianism is sufficient. No more is needed." But you want more. Therefore, you must burn for a Liberty to be enjoyed by others. In other words, you are prepared to expend your scarce resources to secure a value for others. This is our basic definition of altruism again.

The appeal to altruism is also prominent in the pitches on your Movement of the Libertarian Left coupons. In "Our Enemy, The Party," you welcome "donations of encouragement," and ask me to "express my approval of your work" through financial contribution. In the *Manifesto*, you ask people to "express material support for MLL Action!" All of these refer to gifts to MLL over and above the membership fee, with nothing to be delivered by MLL in return.

A similar altruistic tone emerges from much of your *oeuvre*. All this creates a problem of inconsistency of means and ends. A Movement supported by altruistic means is unlikely to consistently seek a libertarian society. In fact, lacking the guide of profit, the supporters of such a Movement are unlikely to consistently pursue *any* long-term goal. Historically, such Movements gravitate toward the ringing Manifesto, the stirring rally, and other forms of action that provide immediate emotional gratification—rather than to forms of action that lead to substantial long-term change. Your activities over the past decade or so seem to have run along these lines.

Of the views you discuss, my own come closest to those you cite in the note on page 24 for Harry Browne—and, of course, the ones for the *Libertarian Connection** (each subscriber may, but needn't, contribute up to four pages per issue to be printed unedited). However, Browne goes overboard in denouncing cooperative action, taking a borscht-belt comic's view of human nature: every wife is a nagging shrew, every business partner is a larcenous leech, *etc.* Cooperative action can be very advantageous if one picks the co-participants prudently, and defines the relationship carefully. The fact that Browne offers "no overall strategy" for social change is no

---

*Membership is $20 for 8 issues (about one year), and entitles you to submit four pages per issue. Still has no Internet presence! Sample is $2.50 from

Erwin S. Strauss
10 Hill Street, #22-L
Newark, NJ 07102

more a valid criticism than is a Christian's complaint that atheism offers no afterlife, or a statist's complaint that agorism offers no benevolent state. The issue isn't offering such things, of course, but delivering them. I've summarized above why I don't think pursuit of your grand strategy will deliver a libertarian society—and even more why it isn't an efficacious use of most people's scarce resources.

The process of "outflanking the state with technology," as you summarize the *Connection* position, isn't a prescription to sit back and wait for this outflanking to happen. Rather, it suggests counter-economic courses of action that might be followed to profit during and after the decline of the state—and, incidentally, to hasten that decline. Your unsupported invocation of the "ingenuity" of the statists to confound these approaches seems defeatist to me. It will take an awful lot of ingenuity, for example, to prevent the spread of weapons of mass destruction. The result of that spread will hardly be pure libertarianism, but it almost certainly will sound the death knell for the state as we know it—if the State doesn't succumb before then.

—Erwin S. "Filthy Pierre" Strauss
March, 1981

REPLY TO FILTHY PIERRE
BY
SAMUEL EDWARD KONKIN III

While the third pole of libertarianism as represented by the *Libertarian Connection* may not have been around as long as Rothbard and LeFevre, to one who entered the Movement during the Great Conversion of 1969 as I did, the three *Connection* stars "Skye D'Aureous," "Natalee Hall" and "Filthy Pierre" were almost as established and respected a view. To an extent, the *Connection* position differs from both and is clearly independent; also, *Connectors* are usually more future-oriented, heavily into technology and market innovations. In fact, if Rothbard seeks to revolutionize us to Liberty and LeFevre to pacify us there—crude simplifications to be sure—*Connectors* want to innovate us there. Since "Skye" and "Natalee" have gone on to do superb work in that area under their real names, Filthy Pierre has become editor of the libertarian APA and the closest to a standard-bearer and spokesperson that the ultra-individualist *Connection* viewpoint has.

To begin with, I'm proud to have Pierre's basic agreement with the New Libertarian "vision." While I have been little influenced *directly* by the *Connection* and its contributors, having read only one issue before he became editor (which was after *NLM*'s publication), some of their better ideas have undoubtedly filtered into general movement lore and I most gratefully acknowledge any that inspired *New Libertarian* and *New Libertarian Manifesto*'s more original and innovative presentations of the libertarian case. So let's check out our few differences.

Pierre is vigilant against the Libertarian Movement re-collectivizing into a potential State. Hear, hear; he is welcome to be a permanent paid watchdog in the pages of *New Libertarian, SNLA* or wherever. I too fear such a possible occurrence and see it already happening in the guise of the LP.

But I am afraid he sees altruism where none was intended, and, I submit, none is present. Discarding one side issue, I consider "public goods" a problem for Chicago economists to dwell on like theologians counting angels on pins.

Pierre does proffer the very service I was looking for in requesting critiques. He discovered an area that I not only was unclear in expressing but that I had not yet realized was a problem. My thanks to his contribution to the clarity of the cause.

What I did make clear is that there is personal freedom and freedom for a society at large—including oneself. Pierre's comment on Browne—with which I almost totally agree!—confirms that. What I failed to make clear is that making *society* freer offers the *immediate* reward of lowering risk. Thus, one judges how much a contribution to agorist activity reduces one's counter-economic risks and contributes accordingly. As we pass through the stages outlined in the *Manifesto*, the advantages become more tangible and obvious if more diffuse, but I do point out that agorist R&D will be transferred to specific industries for their profit and/or reduction of cost—especially insurance and protection.

Where Pierre sees various degrees of "altruism," I see short-term, medium-range, and long-range investment in improving one's surrounding environment—investments that do not clash but are complementary to one's investment in personal freedom and safety

I could not care less about "genetic altruism" and its indulgence.

Pierre does put his finger on the semantic static generated by using terms evolved in politics for the purpose of agorist activism and I hope to see him working further with New Libertarians on developing alternative, clearer labels and popularizing them. (My well-known proclivity for neologizing—coining new words—is prompted precisely to achieve that semantic clarity and to free our language of inappropriate associations.)

The general spread and marketing of weapons of mass destruction may well be coming, but I fail to see how it will have the *critical* effect of abolishing the State. Further debate on this question (opened in *New Libertarian Weekly*) may be warranted.

—Samuel Edward Konkin III
May Day, 1981

This 25th Anniversary Edition of *New Libertarian Manifesto* is set in Century Schoolbook type, a very pleasant and readable font, at 12 points with 13 point leading (SEK3 would approve of the tight layout—no “tasteful white space” for him). Titles are in Book Antiqua. Typesetting, layout, and cover design was performed by Black Dawn Graphics, which has provided services to New Libertarian Enterprises since 1976.

CPSIA information can be obtained
at www.ICGtesting.com
Printed in the USA
BVHW072108310321
603818BV00006B/712

9 780977 764921